TWEEN HOBO

OFF THE RAILS

Written with Alena Smith & drawn with Kate Harmer

GALLERY BOOKS

New York London Toronto Sydney New Delhi

GALLERY BOOKS
A Division of Simon & Schuster, Inc.
1230 Avenue of the Americas
New York, NY 10020

First Gallery Books hardcover edition June 2014

GALLERY BOOKS and colophon are registered trademarks of Simon & Schuster, Inc.

For information about special discounts for bulk purchases, please contact Simon & Schuster Special Sales at 1-866-506-1949 or business@simonandschuster.com.

The Simon & Schuster Speakers Bureau can bring authors to your live event. For more information or to book an event contact the Simon & Schuster Speakers Bureau at 1-866-248-3049 or visit our website at www.simonspeakers.com.

Interior and jacket design by Hum Creative

Jacket art by Kate Harmer   ١٤/٥٤

Manufactured in the United States of America

10 9 8 7 6 5 4 3 2 1

Library of Congress Cataloging-in-Publication Data is available.

ISBN 978-1-4767-4782-8

ISBN 978-1-4767-4784-2 (ebook)

For all my brothers and sisters of the road
(and especially for my BFFL, E. R.)

xoxo T. H.

Ten of us bums up top o' this boxcar—five on
Team Edward, four on Team Jacob, one too
hammered on moonshine to say.

THIS BOOK BELONGS TO:

Hobo Name:

_____

Age

_____

BFFL

_____

Fave Color

_____

Fave Animal

_____

# of Times You've Killed a Guy

_____

# of Times You've Frenched a Guy

————— ————————————————————————————————

Stuff You Can Do with Origami

————————————————————————————————————

Bugs You Hate

————————————————————————————————— —

Bugs You're Cool With

—————————————————————————————————————

Do You Collect Dreamcatchers?

—————————————————————————————————————

Do You Believe in the American Dream?

————————————————————————————————— —

Would You Prefer Squirrel Meat or Vegan Option at My
Bat Mitzvah?

I got hobos (hobos) / in different area codes
(area codes)

TWEEN HOBO

Off the Rails

Three wavy lines on the side of a Pullman car means two hobos got to third in there.

HOBO CODE

On the road, hobos communicate through a system of code. They draw these signs and symbols on the sides of boxcars or water tanks or on the ground near the tracks. Or, if you're a tween hobo, you might draw some on the sidewalk in pink jumbo chalk.

CLASSIC HOBO SIGNS

safe camp

don't give up!

railroad

GO!

get out fast!

Jail

Chain gang

tramps here

you'll get cursed here

See? They're like emoji—but with dirt.

I've pulled off heists, swindles, and emoticons.

A LETTER TO MY FUTURE DAUGHTER

Pineapple Chloe Bieber, Age Negative 15½

My darling Pineapple,

Wassup, future daughter? If you are reading this, then everything went according to plan, and you just came back from competitive horseback-riding to find me and your father, Justin, making heart shapes with our hands to celebrate another sweet-ass year of being married. Congratulations and I love you, family is the most important thing to me.

Now, I want to explain a few things about the book you are holding in your hands. First off, do you know what a book is? It's this thing made of paper that used to exist, but now is only made of electricity (or something, IDK). In the future, when you are reading this, it's probs downloading straight into your brain. So maybe you aren't physically holding it. Regardless, I hope you have a pretty brain, Pineapple Chloe. I hope you have the prettiest brain in your class. And I hope you're the kind of girl who *seems* like an outsider, but is actually just a sexy genius who tends to push people away.

Anywayz: this book. This is my diary. A diary is a very old-fashioned thing, Pineapple. It's kind of like a blog, but no one can see it. It's a secret. That is until you get superfamous and you get a book deal to publish the whole thing, which is what happened to me. See, this diary is a bona fide piece of history in the making. This is the little book that I, your future mother,

4

carried with me on my wild journey as a tweenage train-hopper all across the United States of America. Lots of #folks followed my #ramblings on the roads and rails of the USA as I tweeted about them on Twitter. But only now am I granting access to my supersecret diary as well. As my daughter, I hope you will treasure this book, in old-school or digital format, to be cherished and illegally bit-torrented for generations to come.

In these pages you will learn of my adventures on the road, of the friends I made (and also the frenemies), of the hardships I faced (like getting shingles, or losing my rainbow scrunchie), and of my quest to find the truth about America. Pineapple, the truth about America is not simple. If it was, I prolly woulda just done my Social Studies homework and never hopped the rails in the first place. But now I've been from Poughkeepsie to Missoula, from Albuquerque to Ashtabula, and I can tell you this:

I still believe in the American Dream: work hard and one day you'll get Frenched by a vampire.

Love 4-Eva,
Your Kid-Age Mom from the Past,
Tween Hobo

#1 ♡ ♡ Junior mints ✶ ♡ ♡ ♡ ♡

Feather hair extension

actual feather

knife!

(just in case)

lucky ♣ railroad spike

BIG LEAGUE Bubble gum (chew)

☠ (poison spray)

Silly bandz

Febreze

Origami Paper!

I take life like I take my gummy bears: headfirst.

⇉ JANUARY 7 ⇇

Charlottesville, Virginia

There comes a time in the life of every nine- to twelve-year-old girl when she has to make a choice. Is she gonna open up and swallow the so-called medicine society wants to spoon-feed her? Or will she raise a fist to that nasty stuff and strike out on her own, in search of her own cures—hell, her own poisons?

For me, the crucial moment came yesterday. I was in Social Studies.

My teacher, Mr. Brink, who I happen to know is twenty-eight and on Facebook and in a band and who I happen to have drawn little hearts all around in the yearbook, says it's time to present our individual projects. We're heading into month five of a yearlong "integrated interdisciplinary discovery module," which is about as much fun as it sounds. (My school tries to get creative about everything, but it's like, I don't care if you put me in charge of this "bakery," okay, these cupcakes are made of paper and it's still math. Count me out.) Anyway this year the discovery module is called "What Makes This Country Great." So they keep making us like, split into discussion groups and have "constructive debates" about the Trail of Tears. And now we're supposed to unveil these individual projects. And of course Mr. Brink has to pick me to go first.

Before I go any further, I should tell you a little more about myself. I'm in fifth grade at James Monroe Upper Elementary School in Charlottesville, Virginia. My birthday's in October so I'm recently eleven, which makes me one of the younger, and, I like to think, cuter, kids in my class. I play left wing in soccer, my favorite flavor is watermelon, and my sticker collection is fearsomely eclectic. My bat mitzvah has already been scheduled for a year and a half from now (I'm only half-Jewish, but I'm splitting the bill with another girl from my Hebrew school who's also only half, so that makes one full Jew). I love kittens and puppies and all baby animals, even baby robot animals. I'm brave and strong and I'm super-responsible about my retainer.

And yet I come from a deeply troubled home.

My parents are, basically, zombies. They work all the time, and when they come home, they stalk around with their arms outstretched, unblinking, droning random phrases like "Homework . . . hooommmewooorrkkk" or "Veeegggeettabblleeezz . . ." They also literally *never* put down their phones. I could be lying on the kitchen floor writhing in pain from a *very* painful toe-stub and my mother would still be like, "Wait a sec, hon, I need to take this call." This modern life has sucked out her soul and left her numb.

My dad is something called a cultural commentator, which means he blogs a lot and sometimes goes on the news and discusses things like whether racism still exists. My mom is a psychologist, which means she's very tricky. She has all kinds of theories about raising children, and when she *does* put her phone down for two seconds to talk to me, I never know whether she's saying what she really means or if it's some kind of therapeutic technique.

> Kids today hate Facebook not because our parents can see what we are up to, but because we are forced to see what our parents are up to.

It used to be that the only person I could stand in my family was my big brother. His name is Evan and he's five years older and he used to be supernice to me, like he would teach me how to do stuff and show me cool bugs and high-five me. I wasn't even scared of worms when Evan was around. That's how magnanimous he was. But all that started to change when Evan turned sixteen and started hanging out with the cool kids in his grade and shaved designs into the sides of his head and became a monster. He stopped letting me in his room. And then he went missing.

Steve and Jody, my zombie parents, will not tell me where he went. All they say is he got caught doing some bad things with some bad people, and now he's at a "facility" somewhere "out West" with no internet access and a lot of "guidance." When I press them for more details, such as when the heck he might be coming *home*, their eyes glaze over, their hands rise up, and they start, like, treadmilling into the refrigerator. It's terrifying living with zombies. And I don't know if I'll ever see my brother again.

I like to sneak into Evan's room and look at his stuff when he's not there. Which, now, is all the time. On the ceiling of his bedroom he wrote, in permanent marker, "Life is pointless." A few weeks ago, I went into his room and lay down on his bed and just read those three words, over and over. That's about the time I stopped doing my homework.

But back to Social Studies and What Makes This Country Great. I'm supposed to have a big, superprofessional neon foam board all covered with "research," like Tessa, whose board is plastered with pictures of lightbulbs because her report is on Thomas Edison which, okay, Tessa, that's *one fact*. But when I flip my board around to face the class, it's blank. Well, aside from one random reddish dot, which I think might be blood and if so is definitely *American blood*—but aside from that, I got nothing.

Mr. Brink looks upset, like with his eyes he's saying, *You are not holding up your end of the parent-teacher-student triangle* (which is a phrase that gets thrown at me a lot). Instead, with his mouth, he says, "Where is your project? You had all of winter break to get this done."

I go, "Yeah, but I didn't know what to focus on."

He goes, "That's not a valid excuse. This assignment was very open-ended. You only needed to pick one element of American society or history. Something *you* personally consider important."

I go, "Yeah, but Justin Bieber is Canadian. And One Direction is from England. So I kind of hit a wall."

Tessa goes, "What about the Jonas Brothers?" And I just glare at her like, *bring it*, Tessa. (Sometimes I can't believe that girl is my second-best friend.)

I look back at Mr. Brink, expecting to receive an encouraging hug, or at the very least a patient smile. But he just seems wiped out. And then the fire alarm goes off.

So we all go outside and it's legit *freezing* and I'm like, "Whaaaaaa . . . t?!?!" because I'm used to a pretty controlled climate and this is like, *weather*. And all the girls in my class are jumping around and screaming and videotaping each other on their phones and I look over at Mr. Brink and he's not even *attempting* to supervise. He's just standing off to the side, staring up at the sky.

So I kind of sidle over to my teacher, just to, you know, protect him in case he's in any kind of danger or distress. And when he sees me he goes, "What's up, kid?" And I feel the little Nyan Cat in my soul go riding its rainbow Pop-Tarts double speed.

So I'm like, "Sorry about class." And he goes, "Yeah." And I look at the ground. And he's quiet.

But then he goes, "Fire drills, huh?" And I'm like, "Yeah. They're never real."

And then I realize that somehow we've backed away from the student body and are standing right on the edge of the woods.

Now in the woods behind our school there is a creek. And just over the edge of that creek there's a place where the ground dips down, and then it rises back up again, kind of steeply, and there's a rusty old fence, and just beyond that fence are the railroad tracks. Freight trains come through Charlottesville all the time. They're incredibly long and they take forever to go by. When my mom drives me to school, we have to cross the tracks at an intersection, and if we get there just when a train is arriving, my mom freaks out, because we're already late, and now we have to sit there for twenty minutes as boxcar after boxcar passes in front of our windshield, and I'm missing most of our morning class. Which, I love missing school. So thumbs up, trains.

Once I asked my mom, "Who's on those trains?" And she goes, "Those trains aren't carrying people. They're just carrying stuff. All kinds of stuff that people need from coast to coast. Things like food and clothing. The trains go all over the country, delivering stuff."

I blinked. "Wait a second, So you mean, like, on those trains—there might be—some *jeggings*?"

My mom laughed. "Hey, there might be. You never know." Then she went back to checking her phone.

But back to the edge of the woods, and Mr. Brink. So we're standing there, and it's kind of peaceful, like I can barely hear the other teachers squawking at all the kids to stay in line and "be civilized."

And then I see Mr. Brink has this weird, old leather string twisted around his left wrist, like supercasual, like it's no big deal, when obviously it is a *big deal* when your twenty-eight-year-old teacher is wearing an *accessory* like that. So I go, "Cool bracelet. What is up with that bracelet? I like it. It's somewhat awesome"—trying not to say too much, but at the same time wanting to give it the attention it deserves.

And Mr. Brink goes, "Oh, this? My brother made it."

Now, I have scoured Mr. Brink's Facebook page with the intensity of an OCD-riddled CIA agent, and I never noticed evidence of any siblings whatsoever. So I'm like, "You have a brother?"

And Mr. Brink touches the leather string. "Well. I had a brother."

Terrified, I go, "What happened to him?"

"He disappeared."

"*Seriously?!*" I said, stretching out the word so it included every letter, rather than the simple *srsly?!* I prefer to use in texts. I was about to say, *My brother disappeared too!*, but Mr. Brink spoke first.

"Yeah. Pretty crazy. Went out West. And never came back."

Out *West*? That's where *my brother* went. Out West. It had a certain ring to it. . . . I stared at Mr. Brink. "Why did he go out West? Did he get in trouble?"

"More like he was looking for trouble. He hopped the rails, when we were kids. Never saw him again."

My eyeballs were basically spinning. "What does that mean—*hopped the rails*?"

"He was a train-jumper. It's kind of like hitchhiking, but with trains. You wait for a train to come by and then you run alongside it and catch on. You haul yourself up. And you ride. You can go all over the country, hopping trains. As long as you don't get caught."

I stood very, very still. Then I go, "You can *do that*?"

Mr. Brink snapped out of some moonlit place. He laughed. "Well, *you* can't," he said, attempting to ruffle my hair, though I ducked so he couldn't, because my hair was already at the precise level of messiness that I wanted. "You're—what? Twelve?"

I go, "I'm eleven."

"Okay. So you can't hop trains. You have to go to school."

"I bet I could get a better education hopping trains."

Mr. Brink laughed again.

"No, seriously. I could see America. The *real* America. I could find out the truth about What Makes This Country Great. It would be hands-on learning. And"—I threw this in just to impress him—"I could write about it on my college application."

"You're a little young to be worrying about college, don't you think?"

I nodded. "True. Plus I don't even want to go to college. It's too expensive. And in this economy . . ." I trailed off.

Mr. Brink looked impressed. "For a kid who never does her homework, you sure know a lot. How do you know so much?"

"The internet. Duh."

Mr. Brink shook his head. Then he lets out this big sigh. And he goes, "Man. Who knows?"

"Who knows what?"

"I shouldn't be saying this to you. I could get fired. But you know—you might be right. You could learn a lot out there. Your head is full of all that Bieber nonsense. You're failing school—or maybe school is failing *you*. In a crazy way, it could be good for you—to escape. To explore. To unplug."

In my head I was like, *Uh, yeah, right,* cuz I'd never leave my phone at home, and if I do run away, it'll be straight toward Bieberville, but I kept quiet and let Mr. Brink roll.

He was shaking his head again. "Oh, but don't listen to me. I don't know what I'm saying. I mean—how could I? I never rode the rails. I never took that chance. I didn't have the guts." He shifted the twisted leather string one inch to the left. And looked sad.

It would have been cool if at that exact second we'd heard the train whistle in the distance and a ginormous freight train had come thundering by. It would also be cool if there was a such a thing as Platform 9¾ and I could find it and get whisked away to Hogwarts. But this is real life, so what actually happened was, the principal took out her megaphone and told us the fire drill was over, and we all had to go back inside, and it was annoying because Social Studies was over but I still had to run back to the classroom to get my bag.

But even then, even at that moment when I was shoving my way through the hall to get to the cafeteria for lunch, I knew that everything was different.

I knew which way the wind blew.

I knew I was going to go home that night and pack my bindle (which is what train-jumpers, or "hobos," call their sacks on sticks, see Wikipedia), and the next morning, which was this morning, I knew that when the bus dropped me off at school, I'd fake that I had to go to the bathroom and run to the gym and out to the woods and skip over the creek and climb the fence—and I did. And now I'm here. In my purple jeggings. Waiting for the train.

Not on the tracks, duh, but just shy of them. With my Hello Kitty sleeping bag rolled up tight, and a long stick with a hot-pink Gap pocket-T upcycled into a sack at the end of it, containing all my worldly goods for the journey ahead. And my diary, of course, a copy of which you're reading now, cuz I'm basically the twenty-first-century Anne Frank, if Anne Frank had not died in the Holocaust but instead just peaced out and had a bunch of crazy adventures on the road.*

I'm making my choice. I'm going West, to find the truth: the truth about my brother, the truth about America. And don't freak out, I obvs have my phone so my parents can text me and stuff. Plus I'm on Facebook, Foursquare, Twitter, Tumblr, and Instagram, so I'm not exactly hurtling off the grid. And I brought tampons, in case I *ever* get my period. And Junior Mints. And a knife. And my sticker collection.

But if anything happens to me out on the road, like if I die or whatever? Then bury me 'neath a willow tree. And you can keep my slap bracelets.

OMG!!!!! HERE COMES THE TRAAAAAAIIIINNNN!!!!!!!!!!!!!!!

---

* Which, either way, she would have been a #Belieber.

Tween Hobo @TweenHobo 1/8

I'm a solitary, capable highwayman with a high side ponytail.

....

Tween Hobo @TweenHobo 1/9

All my tattoos will be tramp stamps, regardless of location.

....

Tween Hobo @TweenHobo 1/10

Brother, can you spare a dime? Sister, can I borrow your DVD of *Vampire Diaries, Season 2*?

....

Tween Hobo @TweenHobo 1/11

A hobo's gotta live by the whimsicalities of chance. Which is why I keep my iPod on shuffle.

....

Tween Hobo @TweenHobo 1/12

Sittin' on a log, updatin' my blog.

....

Tween Hobo @TweenHobo 1/13

Found a dead possum in the woods, named her Lily.

....

Tween Hobo @TweenHobo 1/14

If the Biebz ever wanted to ride the rails, I'd show him what for and I'd watch over him as he slept.

....

Tween Hobo @TweenHobo 1/15

My recent Google search history includes poisonous berries, switchblades, and Caboodles.

Tween Hobo @TweenHobo   1/16

If the Lord didn't intend for me to be a rollin' stone, he wouldn't have invited trains—or Heelys.

....

Tween Hobo @TweenHobo   1/17

Need a sip a' cool water so's I kin take my ADD meds.
When I'm on the road I forget my troubles, like how Dad said absolutely no to a vampire-theme bat mitzvah.

⇒ JANUARY 18 ⇐

Philadelphia-ish

I am LOL-ing so hard right now because here I am in a dusty boxcar going nine hundred miles an hour through the dark of night and nobody can tell me it's past my bedtime!!!!

By the light of my Flashlight! app I can see the rusty metal walls of the boxcar, my chipping panda-bear nail art, and the rough, weather-beaten faces of my fellow hobos. So much has happened since I caught my first freight out of town, I just hope my glitter pen doesn't run out trying to scribble it all down.

How can I describe the rush I got from "catching out" on my first try?! I'll just say it was even better than the time I won that free roller-skating pizza party. When the train came roaring into the woods behind my school, I did just what Mr. Brink said: I ran alongside it till I could catch hold of the side, and I tossed my Hello Kitty sleeping bag onto the flatcar bed, and then I just hauled myself up. Skinned my knee pretty bad, but luckily, I brought my Lisa Frank Band-Aids with me :)

There was a rusty ladder on the side of the boxcar, and I climbed it all the way up to the top of the train. And—wow. We were zooming through the woods, faster than the Batman ride at Six Flags, and the wind rushed through my hair with such force that my sparkly headband blew right off (RIP, sparkly headband!!!!). I pumped my fists and twerked a bit because everything was one and everything was infinite. I knew I was leaving Charlottesville and fifth grade far behind. Then I turned around just in time to see that the train was about to enter a terrifying tunnel.

Having just begun to live, I was not ready to die. I threw myself flat down on my belly and grabbed on tight to a rusty latch. We roared into the tunnel and everything went dark and the tunnel filled with thick, black smoke. I was choking and coughing like crazy, and PS, I will *never* say yes to drugs.

Miraculously, I survived! Remind me to say thanks to God at my bat mitzvah! We got out of the tunnel and the sky opened up and I could breathe again, better and deeper than ever before in my eleven years of breathing. I was hooting and hollering and generally getting crunk. And then an even bigger miracle occurred. I met my new best friend.

Wiping the soot out of my eyes, I saw him there, on top of the train. He was just strumming a guitar and being *awesome*. Cautiously, I went over to give him a high five and introduce myself. His name is Stumptown Jim. He wears a blue bandana around his neck, has like twenty scars, is *super* old (he is thirty), and he's been out on the road for a heck of a long time. He is a "socialist," which I guess means he goes to a lot of parties? And he shared his beef jerky with me.

When Stumptown Jim first saw me, skipping along on the top deck of the train, in my purple jeggings and sparkly Uggs, he was a little surprised. But when we "got to talkin'" (his phrase), he realized that we actually have a lot in common. For one thing, we both love freedom. For another—well, okay, the freedom thing is pretty much it. But we're besties.

He's asleep now, across the boxcar from me, but as soon as he wakes up, we'll play another game of MASH. We already played once. Stumptown Jim is going to marry Taylor Swift and have four babies and live in a shack. (Even a shack would be a step up for him.) And if that doesn't happen, we made a pact: we're gonna be Friends with Bindlestiffs.

Stumptown Jim says sometimes an old hobo takes a young'un under his wing and teaches him the ways of the road. I was like, oh, just like Usher and the Biebz! He didn't understand. I pulled up Justin Bieber's Wikipedia on my phone and was like, "There are many things you can teach me, and perhaps, there are some I may be able to teach you." I saw Stumptown's jaw kind of tense up. But then he just nodded, with respect. He is my mentor.

"What are you doin' out on the road, kid?" he asked me. I filled him in on how I'm going to find my brother and bring him home so that my family will magically be fixed and my parents will wake up out of their zombie trance and my brother will be nice to me again. "But in the meantime," I added, "I'm gonna have some fun." He said nothing, but I saw a certified twinkle™ in his eye.

Stumptown Jim has a guitar and he knows lots of songs. He's teaching them to me, but I'm making up my own lyrics.

Go to sleep, you weary hobo
In your shorts that say PRINCESS across the butt . . .

One more thing, before I drift off—this boxcar could use more glow-in-the-dark stars all over it.

Hot-pink nail polish looks good no matter how many fingers you still have.

⤜ HOBO STYLE ⤛

Each time a new bum hoists hisself up on this freight, I'm all, MAKEOVER!!!!! Cuz it's only fun to be a hobo if you can look good doing it. Luckily, there is nothing cooler in the fashion universe these days than the hobo look (spend five seconds googling the Olsen Twins if you don't believe me). Big hobo trends include begging, robbing, dodging John Law—and skinny jeans. In case you ever find yourself riding the rails, here are some basic tips for your fashion survival:

- Rag + sequins = party rag.
- Every hobo needs a blanket that can go from day to night.
- When rations get scarce, you can eat strawberry lip gloss.

- Bindle is the new black.
- The secret to hair this dirty is—don't wash it.
- French braids can really up the wow factor of a filthy beard.

- General rule of thumb? Put a braid in it.
- If it comes in corncob, I want it.
- Boots wit da furrrr: good for hiding out on mountain passes.
- I know this is weird but I secretly wish I had braces and crutches and glasses and was missing an arm.
- I'm not sure what bootlegging is but it sounds supertrendy.
- When twigs and berries get stuck in your hair, think of them as nature's accessories.
- Nobody ever had too many coonskin caps.
- Tween Hobo packing list: spork, jorts, banjitar.

Bottom line: hobos are *all* about layering. Oh, and here's a tip: don't ever get photographed next to a baby wild animal. It will look cuter than you.

Now, any a' you drunken stiffs have a hair thing I can borrow?

Why should I go from rags to riches if rags are on trend?

Tween Hobo @TweenHobo 1/20
Tween Hobo tip: apple juice = pretend whiskey

Tween Hobo @TweenHobo 1/21
Just invented a game called Angry Birds. It involves throwing rocks at telephone wires.

Tween Hobo @TweenHobo 1/22
Soon's I git rid'a my retainer, I'm rippin' out all my teeth, replacin' 'em with gold.

Tween Hobo @TweenHobo 1/23
Traded two stolen cabbages for a Ring Pop. #priorities

Tween Hobo @TweenHobo 1/24
Stumptown Jim's been all the way along the Oregon Trail, and he also searched the world for Carmen Sandiego.

Tween Hobo @TweenHobo 1/25
Foragin' in these woods for berries and such, I'm real careful, cuz my pediatrician said I have a nut allergy.

Tween Hobo @TweenHobo 1/26
Thinkin'a hitchin' my way into town to git my ears pierced.

Tween Hobo @TweenHobo 1/27
Shout out to animal crackers, ridin' around in a box just like me.

Tween Hobo @TweenHobo   1/28

Stumptown Jim and I split the work fair & square: he chops the wood and makes the fire, I update the *Bunheads* wiki.

....

Tween Hobo @TweenHobo   1/29

Wind in my face, creek rushin' by—love goin' on a shopping spree for twigs!

 Tween Hobo   1/30

I'm obsessed with nail art.

They couldn't make an American Girl doll of me cuz it would have to come with a small weapon.

⋛ FEBRUARY 1 ⋚

The Big Apple

Cold here in New York Town. Still I could murder some fro-yo. Round about Newark I realized the train was heading straight for the Greatest City on Earth, the place where they shot all six seasons of *Gossip Girl*—and I got *psyyyyyyccchhhheeeddd*. I'm a pretty sophisticated kid, and here I was, arriving in the international mecca for Great Art and Culture. I was determined to soak in as much of it as possible, and I knew just where to start. So as soon as the passenger train pulled into Penn Station, I jumped out from under the seat where I'd hidden myself and hightailed it to the Disney Store in Times Square.

And it was like, *whoa*. What an afternoon! I can safely report, in case anyone was worried, Art and Culture are *killing it* right now. I hit up the Disney Store, M&M's World, Nintendo World, and of course, American Girl Place. All of them rocked me with their colors, their passion. The only problem is, I spent the whole chunk of change I'd brought along for my journey. So now I have these heart-shaped Minnie Mouse sunglasses, this plush green M&M's guy, and a full set of accessories for Addy, the escaped slave doll from the Civil War era, but I don't have Addy and I don't have any money. Oh, well. This miniature wood-and-metal ice-cream maker has gotta come in handy at some point.

Speaking of Addy, I need to take my Ritalin.

Okay, so there I was, just having a ball, eyeing ladies' pocket-books and wondering how much it costs to go ice-skating in this town, and whether they tase you point-blank if you try to sneak out onto the rink, and suddenly, without warning, my personal party got badly busted up. No, it wasn't that somebody forced me to go to ten museums, which is what happened the one time my parents took me to New York. And no, it wasn't the moment when the lady at the TKTS booth told me, quite heartlessly, that *Shrek the Musical* was not playing on Broadway anymore. It was worse. I ran into my FREAKING AU PAIR.

In case you don't know what an au pair is, let me explain. It's like a babysitter on crack. A normal babysitter lives down the street or something and comes over for a couple hours while your parents go out to dinner. An au pair comes over *from the freaking Netherlands* and *never leaves your house again*, regardless of whether your parents are out to dinner or not!!! She *eats dinner with your family*!!! She *goes on vacation with you*!!! And if she's anything like *my* au pair, she wears inappropriate booty shorts and spends all her time on Skype with her boyfriend in Holland. And her name is Honig. Which she says sounds like "honey" in Dutch. Which, sorry, Dutch. You lost that round.

Okay, so I'm just loitering in the crowded accessories wing of a Forever 21, just innocently plunging my forearms elbow-deep into a giant plastic tub of scrunchies, because it kind of relaxes me, when I hear that shrieking Dutch-accented voice go, "Ah, now the monkey comes out of the sleeve!" I whip around to see Honig, in the flesh, standing there with another tall, blonde Dutch girl who might as well be her identical twin, only they'd be too dumb to pull off a successful *Parent Trap* situation. Both of them are wearing hot-pink pajama bottoms with "I ♡ NY" printed all over, tiny neon tank tops that barely cover their embarrassing boobs, and, because after all it's below freezing outside, cropped faux-fur vests. In short, they look great—but I'm not happy to see them.

Honig grabs me by the ponytail, air-kisses me five times, then goes to her friend, "Hallo, Kaatje, dis is de little *poepje* dat de agency, dey giff me! Dis little *kloothommel*, she run away! But fee find you now, *ja*?" I grimace. Kaatje chortles. Honig whips out her flip-phone. "I call your parents, but I haff no more minutes on de pay-as-you-go. . . . Kaatje, you haff minutes?" Kaatje hurtles through a paragraph or more that I imagine translates basically to "Who cares about this kid, we are on our mandatory one-weekend-off-a-month, we need to hit up H and M and then go to Applebee's to meet up with those sexy freaks on that Italian teen tour." I try to duck away while Kaatje pronounces things, but Honig catches me. "I know what!" she screams. "You come fis us, you haff crazy weekend fis de big girls, *ja*?! Fee get de ears pierced, fee go to de techno club, fee make a short visit to de 9/11 Ground Zero, and den fee go back to Charlottesville, okay?"

As fun as all *that* sounded, I was like, yeah, no. How could I explain my American quest to these Europeans? How could I make them understand that I had heard, nay, *felt* the words "Go West, young man" in my very soul and had not gotten offended at the fact that they were totes sexist but had just done a little of the ol' cut-and-paste so the message said, "Go West, tween of unspecified gender"?! How could I let them know that this was my destiny, that I was not made for classes and homework, but for a life on the open road, with the sky as my teacher, the prairie as my science room, and the train whistle as my bell! I knew full well that my parents might miss me, that I'd probs have to repeat fifth grade, but these are the risks you take when you commit yourself to high-octane rambling. No, I was headed West and there was nothing that could stop me. And I would not return until I had tasted every slice of the American pie—nut allergies be damned.

Plus, I was going to find my brother. I didn't want to mention that to Honig, who would probably just start blathering about how cute my brother is, because she obvs has a giant crush on him, which raises the question of why my parents got a Dutch au pair who's only three years older than Evan and why *Evan* couldn't just be the one to take care of me like he always used to. But I digress. However, it suddenly occurred to me that as a supposedly "adult" member of the household, Honig might have some information as to my brother's whereabouts. I schemed for a second and then said, "Okay, Honig. You got me. I'll come with you. But will you just tell me one thing? Do you know where my brother is?"

Honig blinked. "Oh, *ja*," she said. "He's in de *rehab*."

Rehab?! What the heck is that?! But Honig continued, "He's in de *California*. Vit all de big celebrities. Like James Van Der Beek. Who is Dutch."

California!!! MY BROTHER'S IN CALIFORNIA?!?! Well, conveniently, so is Justin Bieber! I now had every reason in the world to get out there, out to that golden West, by whatever means necessary.

So just as Kaatje got out her flip-phone so Honig could rat me out to my mom and dad, I made a break for it. Just darted and swerved like crazy out of Forever 21 and through Times Square, narrowly avoiding a collision with the real-life Arby's oven mitt, pausing to give the real-life SpongeBob a courteous high five, and the next thing you know I was at Port Authority, hopping a bus bound for Freehold with Stumptown Jim. But I wasn't planning to stay in New Jersey for long. If one thing was clear to me now it was that I needed to leave the gloomy East behind, as far and as fast as I possibly could.

(Oh, and if you're wondering how I got so independent, fact is, aside from my parents and my au pair I'm basically an orphan.)

Heart-shaped sunglasses, bound for glory.

Tween Hobo @TweenHobo   2/2
I'm obsessed with One Direction—westward ho!

....

Tween Hobo @TweenHobo   2/3
Holdin' onto the side of a westbound freight ain't so hard as holdin' onto a middle-school relationship.

Tween Hobo @TweenHobo   2/4

Only one way to stop a nosy railroad cop: atomic wedgie!

....

Tween Hobo @TweenHobo   2/5

As you go deeper into Ohio, the apple pies get bigger, the ice cream richer, the Razor scooters more cutting-edge.

....

Tween Hobo @TweenHobo   2/6

Not to be a Judy Moody but I'm tired of all these knife fights.

....

Tween Hobo @TweenHobo   2/7

Betcha six Buffalo nickels Selena Gomez can't whittle!

....

Tween Hobo @TweenHobo   2/8

Just unlocked the Three Miles from the Edge of Town badge on Foursquare.

....

Tween Hobo @TweenHobo   2/9

Railroad cop called me a no-account rascal but I have a Twitter account, duh.

....

Tween Hobo @TweenHobo   2/10

Seems like I've always known vagrants, revolutionaries, and how to do the Soulja Boy dance.

....

Tween Hobo @TweenHobo   2/11

Nothing shakes up life in a little town like a traveler passing through with some radical ways of tying her T-shirt up so her midriff shows.

Time moves slow on these nighttime trains; luckily I made a bunch of sweet YouTube playlists.

TWEEN HOBO'S HARD-TRAVELIN' YOUTUBE PLAYLIST

Pokémon Dance Party
Woody Guthrie, "Ludlow Massacre"
Miley Cyrus Takes a Bong Hit of Salvia
Miley Cyrus Twerking in a Unicorn Onesie
Tennessee Ernie Ford Sings "Sixteen Tons"
Goats Screaming Like Humans—Ultimate Compilation
Banana Song—Ten-Hour Loop
Hamster on a Piano (Deep Cut)

Add Your Own Favorites!!!

Folks say YouTube's gonna take over TV, but I'll tell ya what beats YouTube: the good old prairie sky. #notreally #iwish #imsobored

You had me at beans.

⇒ FEBRUARY 13 ⇐

Chagrin Falls, Ohio

I was nervous all day today because, aside from the fact that I'm four foot nine and riding a red-ball freight with no supervision, I knew tonight was going to be huge: Stumptown Jim invited me to come eat mulligan stew down in Hobo Jungle. Which is basically like a really cool outdoor pizza party, but with hobos, and instead of pizza, a big, disgusting soup made of cabbage and squirrel meat. I said, "I like my soup like I like my Bieber: pipin' hot and full'a beans." And he said, "Everyone will be there." So I knew I needed to make a good impression.

I spent like an hour wondering what to wear and then finally accepted that I only had one option, because I didn't bring any other clothes. Luckily the outfit I chose to run away in is pretty stylin', not to mention versatile: I mean, is there any event or occasion where you *can't* just show up in sparkly UGGs, purple jeggings, a plaid shirt, and a bowler hat? Accented with panda-bear nail art and a jaw-dropping collection of Silly Bandz? Still, though, tonight was really special and the pressure was on, so I whipped my BeDazzler out of its holster and added about fifty sequins to my jeggings. Then I got melancholy because I realized, out here on this lonely road, I have Traveling Pants—but no sisters :(

Well, I shouldn't have spent even a second feeling sad. Because tonight was so much fun it'd break the party-hat emoji on my phone if I sent you a text about it. I made a ton of new friends and even a couple frenemies. So many hobos kept coming up to me and Jim and introducing themselves, offering us bites of lard and sharing tips about how to stop the bleeding from a wound with hunks of wet mud, that I'm worried I might get a reputation as the second-fiddle Gretchen Wieners to Stumptown Jim's queen bee. Especially since I kept whispering to Jim that we should start a Burn Book. He agreed, but he thought I meant an instructional pamphlet about starting fires. When actually, duh, I meant a secret notebook where you write down really mean things about people. (See next page.)

Overall, it was a great night. (Although something tells me the stew was neither kid-tested nor mother-approved.) The old hobos and I sat around the fire and talked of many things. A fella by the name of Tin Cap Earl got serious for a minute and asked me what I was doing out on the road. I didn't feel ready to tell him about my brother. What I said instead was that I was on a quest to find out What Makes This Country Great. Everybody looked kind of thoughtful. He said, well, you'll be out here a long time then. Good luck to ya, kid.

And OMG I think this guy Hot Johnny Two-Cakes is anorexic. He didn't even finish his beans. (For more about Hot Johnny and the rest of the hobos, check out my Burn Book!! Next page!!)

Me and Stumptown Jim are the Mean Girls of the hobo community.

⚡MY HOBO BURN BOOK⚡

Toothpick Frank

One of the grossest guys I've ever seen, and don't forget Kevin R. is in my class. Also rude. Kept talking about "going down to the cathouse" and refused to invite me even though I love kittens. They call him Toothpick Frank because he wears this weird curving, skinny, yellowish bone on a chain around his neck, which he says is the bone of a "raccoon's dick" (his words!) and it's Nature's answer to the toothpick. It's hard to believe, but this is the least disgusting thing about Toothpick Frank.

Tin Cap Earl

I actually have nothing mean to say about Tin Cap Earl, because what kind of shade can you throw at a guy who *immediately* offers to teach you how to Dougie? Of course I already know how to Dougie, but still, it's the thought that counts. Tin Cap Earl has amazing style and distinct second-best-friend potential. (Sorry, Tessa—you might get demoted.) And there's really nothing cooler than his hat. Which is literally a saucepan.

Blind Hank

Blind item: I know a blind guy. Okay, fine, it's Blind Hank. He's only blind in one eye, but unfortunately the other eye is missing. I'm psyched because as soon as I get to know him a little better, I'm gonna get all Miracle Worker on him and teach him how to spell *water*. Which is something that's been high on my bucket list. Oh—that reminds me: top item on my bucket list—get a new bucket.

Whiskey Bob

Seems to be a bit of a workaholic, if his job is staggering around drunk in a filthy clown suit. When I offered to French-braid his beard, he just laughed and threw some beans in my face. And then puked. He's not invited to my bat mitzvah.

Floyd Caboose

If I made a movie about Floyd Caboose, it would be called *I Don't Know How He Does It*. The guy has no legs. Stumptown Jim says Floyd falls off the train a lot, but then somehow shows up again at the next station. I like him cuz he's the only one shorter than me.

Salt Chunk Annie

A motherly, weather-beaten lady who introduced herself as a "Woman of the Night." I told her I was more of a "Twilight Girl" myself. She said if I ever needed work, I could come to her.

Apparently she runs the cathouse. I was like, yeah, no thanks, I love kittens but not like it's my *job*. She was nice, though. And not at all stingy with the jerky.

Hot Johnny Two-Cakes

Hot Johnny Two-Cakes. Hot Johnny Two-Cakes. Can't stop saying his name for some reason. Not sure why. I definitely don't have a crush on him. I mean, come on. Why would I have a crush on a weird emo guy who just sat by the fire and had cool hair and never even talked to me? Yeah, right. Plus I don't think the name of my future daughter Pineapple Chloe Bieber could really turn out to be Pineapple Chloe Two-Cakes. That would just be so funny if that did happen. I wonder what kind of cakes they are. I like his jeans. I think maybe I hate him?

I've started to get the feeling that riding the rails can make you meaner'n'a rattlesnake. And I mean like a really popular rattlesnake.

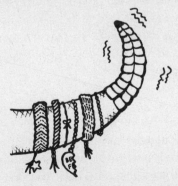

Wheresoe'er I ramble, the boys are SO immature :(

⋛ VALENTINE'S DAY ⋚

The truth is, I don't care about Valentine's Day. I mean, why should I? It's just a fake holiday anyway, probably invented by the guys at the Candy Heart Company to unload their product on the masses, and of all the candies in the world, I think we can agree that those valentine hearts with little messages on them are pretty far down the chain tastewise. Although they would make cute earrings, but that's not the point of candy, last time I checked. The point of candy is to give you a full-body joy-blast and make you feel like you've taken a productive business trip around the world on the back of a unicorn whose hair gets in your mouth sometimes but luckily it's made of spun sugar. Which, candy hearts? Not even close. They taste like floor.

The other reason I don't care about Valentine's Day is that I already found the love of my life, the man who will receive my final rose, and his name is Justin Drew Bieber and he is a Canadian song-stylist, and when I die, they will bury us beside one another in matching purple sweatshirts. So from now till whenever I stand at that altar with Justin and give myself to him, all Valentine's Days and drive-ins and proms and courtside basketball seats and hayrides and whatnot are, essentially, a wash.

Sidebar:

You know the way that little girls say *purple*? It's so cute. They can't really pronounce the *r* so they're like, "poy-puh." I'm going to be such a proud mom one day in the future when tiny Pineapple Chloe Bieber points to my and her dad's matching zip-up hoodies and goes, "Poy-puh." Awwww. And then I'll be like, "Power down your Google Brain Chip, sweetheart. It's time for bed." And then my husband and I will pop open a good bottle of Mountain Dew and look out at the grand vista of our hillside ranch, which will hopefully still be a nice vista even after global warming, and we won't even need to talk, we'll just enjoy the warm silence of two best friends with benefits who have also exchanged holy vows and imprinted on each other and been through a *lot*.

Also I hope my mom will live close by.

So considering how *minuscule* of a crap I give about Valentine's Day, it's kind of *ironic* that Hot Johnny Two-Cakes is refusing to be a guest on my podcast just because it happens to be February 14. I know *hate* is a strong word, but I like strong words. And I hate Hot Johnny. He's a conceited emo poser whose jeans are too skinny, and the only reason I cry when he plays the banjo is because he *sucks* at it. I don't even especially *care* if he's a guest on my podcast, I just thought it might be semi-interesting to interview him about his eyes and hair and stuff. Oh, well. I'm doing the podcast without him. Kicking off with this Gotye cover. Now you're just some hobo that I used to know :(. . .

Longest relationship I ever had was four days. It was with a pebble I was carrying around.

Tween Hobo @TweenHobo   2/15
Sippin' Cran·Grape from a dead man's boot.

....

Tween Hobo @TweenHobo   2/16
Soon as this train pulls outta the station, Stumptown Jim and I call same seats.

....

Tween Hobo @TweenHobo   2/17
I don't just like beans—I *like* like 'em.

....

Tween Hobo @TweenHobo   2/18
I'm always taking candids of Toothpick Frank and he acts mad but then he goes, "Post it, you bastard."

....

Tween Hobo @TweenHobo   2/19
Every time I hear a wolf a-howlin' in the woods, I kind of assume it's a sexy, magical Native American werewolf.

....

Tween Hobo @TweenHobo   2/20
Taylor Swift is perfect cuz she knows she has her flaws! I'm perfect too even tho I set that barn on fire :/

Tween Hobo @TweenHobo   2/21

O Bieber Where Art Thou?

....

Tween Hobo @TweenHobo   2/22

Hobo Willow Smith: "I whip my BEARD back and forth, I whip my BEARD back and forth." LOL

....

Tween Hobo @TweenHobo   2/23

Trees throw shade but I don't take it personally. #hey-oh

....

Tween Hobo @TweenHobo   2/24

Hot Johnny Two-Cakes and I are playing a game where he pretends he never got my text and I pretend I'm not plotting to murder him.

....

Tween Hobo @TweenHobo   2/25

I lost a tooth today. Toothpick Frank lost five.

ZACHARY TAYLOR: HOTTIE PRESIDENT

Even though I'm skipping school to become a full-time drifter, I recognize that I am still a kid, and, as the saying goes, "I need structure." Plus, like I told Mr. Brink, I'm out here on the road to get an education that'll beat anything we ever did in school (except for when we got to make up those little raps about science). So I'm gonna be like my own annoying babysitter and *make* myself do homework. Like reports and stuff. So my first report is about:

My Favorite President

My favorite US president ever is Zachary Taylor, because he sounds most like he was a member of a boy band. Here are some facts about our Cutest President Ever:

· Fact: Zachary Taylor was known as Old Rough and Ready— but I like to call him Z-Tay.
· Fact: It must have been so sad when Hottie President Z-Tay died and the next president was non-boy-band-eligible Millard Fillmore.
· Fact: Hottie in Chief Zachary Z-Tay Taylor was the twelfth US president. Also, I am almost twelve. Coincidence? IDK.
· Fact: Abraham Lincoln was a vampire hunter. Zachary Z-Tay Taylor was just a hottie with a body.
· Fact: They make a million boring movies about Abraham Lincoln, but still not ONE about America's Hottest President, Zachary Z-Tay Taylor!
· Fact: America's not ready for a Z-Tay biopic. The combination of X Games skate moves and Whig politics is just too hot to handle.

I'll conclude with the classic Z-Tay lyric: "The way that you flip your hair gets me overwhelmed . . . I don't know-ow-ow / If I should allow slavery in the western states."

♡ ♡ ♡ Z-TAY ♡ ♡ ♡

Old hobos speak of a mystical Pepsi that was
Crystal Clear . . .

OLD HOBOS SAY THE DARNEDEST THINGS

Sittin' around the campfire a'night with my homeys, who are old as hell, I hear them talk of days gone by, when they were young, like the 1990s and stuff. Most of the time I don't have a clue what they're yappin' about, and don't care, but once in a while they'll speak of a thing so odd and fanciful It can't help but catch my attention.

Like what the crap is Pearl Jam??

And a gal named Jem who was Truly Outrageous?
And a Noid that was to be Avoided. . .
And a Melon who went Blind . . .
And a gymnast they called Dominique Dawes . . .
And a Young Gun they called Brad Renfro . . .
And a Stylish Emporium known as Contempo Casuals . . .
And how they used to collect Absolut ads . . .
And a talkie called *I Know What You Did Last Summer* . . .
And a band called Soul Asylum, which I YouTubed them? And now I'm like, *whoa*.
Other questions:

- Who in the heck are Bill and Ted??
- What in tarnation is a laser disc?!?!?!?!
- Did you know there once lived two rappers by the names of Salt and Pepper, and they had a song called "Soup"?!?!?!

- What is this quaint saying I hear bandied about—"I ain't afraid a' no ghosts"???
- There's something called a "Blowfish"? And a "Hootie"?

Old hobos talk of a band called Counting Crows—bet I'd like 'em, cuz guess what I did all morning.

Tween Hobo @TweenHobo   3/1

It was down by the locomotive roundhouse in Des Moines one strange afternoon that I awoke from my nap like—wait, where's my rainbow scrunchie?

....

Tween Hobo @TweenHobo   3/2

Tryin' to make my voice all deep and scratchy so I sound like an old hobo (or Miley Cyrus).

....

Tween Hobo @TweenHobo   3/3

Took a puff off Floyd Caboose's pipe, got a total head rush.

....

Tween Hobo @TweenHobo   3/4

How long is too long to wait for a text from a tadpole?

....

Tween Hobo @TweenHobo   3/5

That awkward moment when you're ridin' freight with thirteen bums and one of 'em falls off . . .

....

Tween Hobo @TweenHobo   3/6

Railroad bull called me a lousy scamp. Still got it!

....

Tween Hobo @TweenHobo   3/7

It's a terrible loneliness comes over me a-nights, knowin' them Stars Are Just Like Us.

....

Tween Hobo @TweenHobo   3/8

I can't be dolin' out homework pills to every Tom, Dick, and Jayden.

Tween Hobo @TweenHobo   3/9

How do you indicate "nut allergy" in smoke signals? #Worst-CaseScenario

....

Tween Hobo @TweenHobo   3/10

Don't make jokes about guys who play the spoons. #TooSpoon

....

Tween Hobo @TweenHobo   3/11

Emoji story of my night: 🔥🤸🚔 (campfire, gymnastics, arrested)

 Tween Hobo   3/12

So, this happened.

So broke I had to put my retainer in hock.

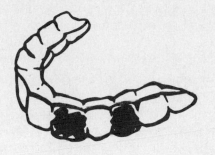

⇒ MARCH 14 ⇐

Kansas City, Missouri (Not Kansas? #wtf)

Been out on the road two months now and I owe debts all over *SimCity*. In Chicago I started a lemonade stand, and for a minute I thought I could have it all. But while I was climbing the corporate ladder, one of the acorn babies in my shoebox rolled away. Plus demand dried up when neighborhood parents realized I was just rinsing out my yellow watercolor brush and selling the results to their kids.

Now according to Stumptown Jim, here's the difference between hobos, tramps, and bums: Hobos want to work. Tramps are just looking for adventure and good times, and bums, well, they mainly drink and steal (hotlink: Toothpick Frank). If you want to get technical about it, I'm somewhere between a hobo and a tramp (it's a spectrum). But right now, in my circumstances, I'd do just about anything to turn an honest dime.

Here's the difference: Tramps roam. Bums steal. Hobos work. And Tween Hobos #twerk

See, you'd never guess it by my blinged-out strawberry Ring Pop, but I'm flat broke. Folks, I'm not looking for a get-rich-quick scheme—I'd settle for a plain old get-less-poor scheme. Trouble is, there ain't no work to be found. And it's not as if I don't work hard. I mean, when it comes to pretending to be a chimney sweep? I'm a workaholic!

But I won't ask for your pity. I will present you with the facts, and you can make up your own mind as to whether or not there is someone with two thumbs who has not been given a fair shot by society and it's *this tween*. Yes, my dudes, the deck is stacked. And the game's not Yu-Gi-Oh! The game is Life.

As soon as I realized I'd spent my last nickel on that plush green M&M's guy at the Disney Store in Times Square (the plush green M&M's guy who now just stares at me with desperate eyes), I got serious. I basically took *myself* to Take Your Daughter to Work Day. I pulled down the shades of my mental conference room, flipped on my mental multimedia projector, and kicked off a full-scale mental PowerPoint presentation. Unfortunately, when the first slide clicked on, it said "Job Search" and I got so bored I had to grab my sticker collection and use two oversize banana stickers to tape my eyelids open so I'd stay awake. Then I looked so funny that I had to take out my phone for documentation, and post a selfie of me with these eyelid banana stickers, and then I had to take another picture of my feet in the rainbow-striped toe socks I was wearing, and then I had to skid around the boxcar for a while. Turns out I'm amazing at skidding. Can you get paid for that?

Anyway, I was attempting to snap the perfect shot of myself midskid when Tin Cap Earl lowered himself down into the boxcar from the roof. He asked if he could borrow my phone to check something called Grindr, which, I don't really get how a phone can be a coffee appliance, but, okay, Tin Cap Earl. I told him I'd trade him my phone for some career advice. He said make it the phone plus one of those banana stickers and you got yourself a deal. We did our special Dr Pepper hand-slap routine and shook on it.

Tin Cap Earl's first tip was this: Every hobo's got a thing he does real well so he can make a little scratch from time to time. A craft, a trade. What's yours? And I said, friendship bracelets. But I'm low on string.

Then he asked me, what are your credentials? I told him how I got a Penguin Level Two badge in figure skating. Which he said probably makes me overqualified for most positions.

Then we got into a long discussion about something he called the Creative Class, which sounds like it would involve Magic Markers and kids with severe ADD but is apparently a whole "twenty-first-century economic reality" where a lot of grown-ups with fancy degrees do endless amounts of writing and graphic design and stuff for next to nothing. They're always working for free, which I guess is why they call them freelancers. It started to dawn on me that *I* was a member of the Creative Class and that I had been forking over my valuable Tween Hobo™-brand goods left and right to the Man, such as yesterday when I slam-dunked another Google novelty logo with peace signs, a flag, ten yin-yangs, a SpongeBob, and WHAT ELSE DO YOU NEED, GOOGLE,

JUST PAY ME. Or how 'bout the fact that Instagram could up and sell most of my pics as advertisements for blurry zoomed-in spiderweb companies. Well, I was off that merry-go-round. It was time for this little hobo to *monetize*.

So I rolled up my sleeves (which is hard to do in a tank top) and asked Tin Cap flat out if he knew of anybody, anywhere, who was hiring. He said he'd heard of a farm nearby that would pay you minimum wage to lay out sprinkler pipes in their cornfields. (Thanks to global warming, it hasn't rained in weeks, and the farmers are more or less freaking out. The corn is def not as high as an elephant's eye, unless that elephant is lying down flat on an IKEA futon in the middle of the afternoon because he's so depressed.) I asked Tin Cap why he didn't go hit up this farm himself and he said, "TMI" (Too Much Irrigation). I agreed that working in the hot sun didn't sound superfun, but then I heard the word *sprinkler* and perked up. Maybe the farmer would have a Slip 'N Slide.

Spoiler alert: The farmer did not have a Slip 'N Slide. The farmer also refused to hire me. He said I should go start a lemonade stand. I said been there, done that. He said child labor was illegal in America last time he checked, and he would never hear of such a thing. So I had no choice but to walk away as a bunch of Mexican dudes lined up to hand over thirty-two pounds of fresh-picked tomatoes for about fifty cents each.

Also, turns out cornfields can be a *li'l* tricky to find your way out of.

―――――――――――――

My next shot at the American Dream was more entrepreneurial. It was so businesslike I needed shoulder pads. At the same time, it's funny to me that I didn't think of it sooner. I guess it was just one of those ideas that you're so close to, you actually need to take a few steps *back* before you can see it. There I was, a red-blooded capitalist tween with flexible afternoons and a dynamic group of friends (hobos). What other choice was there? I started a babysitters' club.

Well, starting the club was fun (see following for more details), but I'm not sure we're ever going to turn a profit. There's just no honest work in this two-horse town. Can't find work, can't find food, can't find my purple jeggings :(Maybe it's time to move on. Maybe a kind old lady with failing sight will pay me a nickel to recap some YouTube vids. Maybe I should start a Kickstarter . . . for my life.

It's hard to pull yourself up by your bootstraps when you're wearing UGGs.

HOBO BABYSITTERS CLUB

Here's how my hobo babysitters club works: you make one phone call, you reach six hobos, any of which might be free to come handle your kids. The members of the club are:

Stumptown Jim (President)

I let Jim be president even though the club was my idea, because everyone respects him. It's his job to lead the meetings, and also every now and again to kind of emotionally look out into the distance like he's seeing all the way to that big hobo babysitters club meeting in the sky. He also came up with the idea for the Kid-Kits (more on that later). Jim's signature accessory is a blue bandana. He's kind of a tomboy (really, even for a thirty-year-old man) and, like Kristy from the real BSC, he'll probably never need to wear a bra.

Tween Hobo (Vice President)

I made myself veep of the club like Claudia Kishi, not because she is my favorite (Stacey is my favorite, more on that later), and not because I am Asian American (as stated, I am half-Jewish), but because, like Claudia, I am addicted to SNACKS. It is my job to provide hella candy at every meeting, which, to tell you the truth, I usually don't, because (a) we are hobos and never have any food, and (b) if I do get candy, I'm *probably* not going to tell anybody about it. But I did use my glitter pens and a stack of cardboard to make each club member a personalized

begging sign to hold up at freeway intersections that says Will
Work for SweeTarts.

Tin Cap Earl (Secretary)

Tin Cap is club secretary because he has really good handwrit-
ing. (I learned this the other night when we went out graffiti
bombing and I saw him throw up a dope piece on the side of
an overpass. His tag is Steady Hustlin with a bunch of zigzags
and arrows coming out of all the letters.) He's in charge of the
club notebook, where we all have to write down little accounts
of the jobs we do, like whether the kids behaved, whether the
parents were nice, and if for example there was any #soup. We
haven't gotten a single job so far, but Tin Cap went ahead and
tagged the cover of the notebook.

Blind Hank (Treasurer)

You have to assume when you set up a hobo babysitters club
that whoever the treasurer is will probably steal all the money.
That's why I gave the job to Blind Hank: I figured he can't see
the shoebox where we keep the cash, so we can just steal all
the money from him. Unfortunately Blind Hank overheard me
explaining this logic to the other guys, so now he's onto me, and
his feelings are hurt. Plus that shoebox used to be my cardboard
dollhouse where my acorn babies lived, so now my acorns are
homeless. Which is just sad.

Toothpick Frank (Alternate Officer)

Believe me, I was *not* psyched about letting this guy in the club. He's drunk and mean and he smells like 9/11. It's one thing to send a brave, humble, modern-day folksinger type like Stumptown Jim over to tend to some children; it's quite another to send a confirmed psychopath like Toothpick Frank. But Jim said we had to let him in on account of Frank has been feeling left out ever since I hopped the train and became Jim's new BFFL. Apparently they used to sit together at campfires, and now Jim always sits with me? I didn't want to start the whole Mean Girls drama up again so I just caved. But he better D.A.R.E.–To Keep Kids off Moonshine.

Hot Johnny Two-Cakes (Associate Member)

You know how the regular Baby-Sitters Club had one member, Logan Bruno, who was a boy? Well that's kind of the role played in our club by Hot Johnny Two-Cakes. Even though all the other hobos are technically boys too. And even though Hot Johnny Two-Cakes, with his hair and everything, kind of looks like a girl. I don't know. It's confusing. Things are always confusing when it comes to Hot Johnny Two-Cakes. Let's just say he adds a little spice.

So, that's our club. We meet every day from 3:30 p.m. to 5:30 p.m. down in Hobo Jungle. Our phone is a tin can. The Kid-Kits, which we take along on babysitting gigs to give the kids something fun and possibly educational to do, consist of one arrowhead and a Zippo lighter. Oh–and for the record, Stacey is my favorite because she has diabetes and I have shingles.

OMG, we're getting our first call!!

Hello, Babysitters Club! . . .Yes, we have one sitter available—however he is drunk and has no teeth, is that okay? . . . Hello? (shakes tin can)

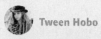 Tween Hobo · 3/16

The Babysitters Club had an unproductive meeting last night.

I can't help it—I'm jealous of ladybugs.

⋟ BUG TALK ⋞

Being a hobo means being outside a lot. I'm technically an indoor kid so I'm not used to this at all. But with my new lifestyle, I've learned a lot about bugs and other animals. Here's some straight talk about the facts.

- Spiderwebs: hate the players, love the game.
- If a snail leaves a little bit of slime on your hand, you are "going out."
- Lightning bugs are my jam.
- If there was a soccer team for bugs, daddy longlegs would volunteer to coach. He's just that kind of dude.
- Crickets get crunk.

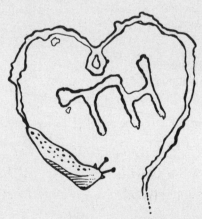

BIRD POOP
(*poop* means "facts" #LOL)

- I blame crows for almost everything.
- In a pinch, you can text via woodpecker.
- Meadowlarks need to chillax.
- HelloGiggles rejected my listicle about whip-poor-wills.

RANDOM ANIMAL FACTS

- Reckon I'd name a pet squirrel Juliet.
- I used to be BFFs with a gopher, but she scurried away.
- Stray dogs are not *necessarily* looking for love.
- A murder of crows. A warren of rabbits. A sparkle of bronies.
- Know what's top-notch? A sea horse.

- A deer that you shoot will respect you because game recognize game.
- Rainy day activity: upcycle a worm into a pet.

With birds you can't tell the difference between a tweet and a retweet.

Tween Hobo @TweenHobo   3/17

Kansas City, preacherman boards the train, says the best book of all is God's words. And I'm all, okay, so Stephenie Meyer is GOD. LOL.

....

Tween Hobo @TweenHobo   3/18

Know what always bucks my spirit? Unicorn stuff.

....

Tween Hobo @TweenHobo   3/19

Crossin' thru the Great Plains I'm all, this is how flat my chest is :(

....

Tween Hobo @TweenHobo   3/20

Lookin' up at the moon on a cold prairie night, I swear I saw the Biebz shinin' down on me. . . .

....

Tween Hobo @TweenHobo   3/21

Johnny Two-Cakes and I robbed the post office and they didn't even have any Disney stamps. #fail

....

Tween Hobo @TweenHobo   3/22

It sucks when the boy you like gets put in a different section gang.

....

Tween Hobo @TweenHobo   3/23

If it was rainin' soup, I couldn't buy myself a tin spoon—but if it was raining glitter. I'd be *psyched*.

....

Tween Hobo @TweenHobo   3/24

Kind lady at the local greasy spoon offered to buy my breakfast, but they didn't have Frosted Mini-Wheats so I was like kthxbai.

Tween Hobo @TweenHobo   3/25

Sometimes the most beautiful thing is just a plastic bag, blowing around on the tracks. I'm kidding, that sucks.

....

Tween Hobo @TweenHobo   3/26

If you don't feel like watching a fashion show, then you shouldn't be up on top of the train.

There are still one or two facts I don't understand about mermaids. Like are they real or not?

⌇MERMAIDS ⌇

When we crossed the mighty Mississippi it mostly made me think about a very important subject, which is
MERMAIDS.

What's this mess about mermaids being real?

I keep hearing this stuff about mermaids being real, and I'm like, is that true? Is that correct? What's the scuttlebutt here on this one?

I would like to be a mermaid in the mighty Mississippi. I would either float on a raft or just swim.

I can get pretty close to being a mermaid. What I do is I stick my legs in a sack and flop around like "Up where they WALK / Up where they RUN / Up where they PLAY all day in THE SUN" . . .

You're wondering why I've been so quiet today. Well, that's what happens when you sell your voice to a sea witch for legs, DUH.

This has been a report on mermaids. Real? Or not? I hope we clear the mess up soon.

AN EMAIL FROM MR. BRINK

Today I got an email from my teacher!!!! Reproduced here in its entirety. All redactions courtesy of Harriet the Spy, I mean Harriet the NSA Surveillance Systems administrator.

From: mr_brink@XXXXX.edu
To: tweenhobo12@XXXXX.biz
Sent: 3/28, 2:15 PM
Subject: We Miss You

Hey kid,
Parent-teacher conferences are coming up and I don't know what I'm going to tell your folks, because you haven't been to school in almost three months. I'm pretty concerned that you might have taken some of my words the wrong way, like for example when I told you about train-hopping. That was kind of a "do not try this at home" situation. But I guess I didn't make that sufficiently clear.

Anyway, we miss you around here. . . . Tessa and the other girls built a little shrine to you, with pictures and Post-it notes, and they spend every recess inside just holding hands around the shrine and crying. It's actually kind of creepy.

I should also let you know that in your absence, the fifth-grade class has been lucky enough to acquire a class pet. He is a very tiny turtle, and we haven't named him yet because everyone agreed it wasn't fair to name him without your valuable input. He is so tiny that his head is smaller than a strawberry. So put your thinking cap on, and we hope you come back soon—because this little guy needs a name.

Also, you owe three months' worth of homework.

Wherever you are, be safe . . . and, hey, if you run into my brother—say hi for me. (I'm kidding. Kind of.)

Worriedly yours,
Mr. Brink
P.S. xxxxxxxx juice-box xxx.

for scale! ↑

Tween Hobo @TweenHobo   3/29
This world's short on mercy and long on Chipmunks ringtones.

Tween Hobo @TweenHobo   3/30
Townspeople can be really exclusive.

Tween Hobo @TweenHobo   3/31
This world ain't nothin' but bums, thieves, and frenemies.

Tween Hobo @TweenHobo   4/1
That thing where you fall down a well

Tween Hobo @TweenHobo   4/2
That thing where you use the whole buffalo

Tween Hobo @TweenHobo   4/3
That thing where all your homeys get the pox

Tween Hobo @TweenHobo 4/4
Blood on the tracks. No, wait, that's just drips from my smoothie.

....

Tween Hobo @TweenHobo 4/5
If I was rich, I'd be all, "Six Flags, Jeeves, and step on it."

....

Tween Hobo @TweenHobo 4/6
Just because I'm a hobo don't mean I can't get a real classy ankle tattoo of a baby Taz.

....

Tween Hobo @TweenHobo 4/7
That thing where you lose a game of gin to a man named Soapy

....

Tween Hobo @TweenHobo 4/8
You know—I got enough troubles. I don't give an eff where Waldo is.

There's just something extradelicious about stolen pie.

⋛ APRIL 9 ⋚

Omaha, Nebraska

Are you there God? It's me, Tween Hobo. Something really upsetting™ happened the other day. I picked up my Hobo Burn Book to write a thumbs-down review of some roughnecks who jumped on in Mason City, and the book fell open to reveal a page that I did *not* write—a page that was written, in crude scrawl—about *me*.

In words that will haunt me till my dying day or at least my junior prom, the troll said, *What the what. A hobo with a cell phone and a data plan? Born rich and chooses the hobo life? Get off the train before you hurt yourself, princess. TWEEN HOBO IS A FAKE.*

I read it over and over. Then I just sat there for twenty minutes with my knees pressed up against my chest, trying to look sad. I mean, I *felt* sad, but it's also important to *look* sad. But then nobody was there to see me, and I couldn't Instagram myself because I needed both hands to hug my knees.

It was clear that I had to do something, fast, to prove myself to this loser whose opinion I couldn't care less about. I had to figure out what a Real Tween Hobo Move would be, and then make that Move. So I go up to Stumptown Jim and I go, "What's a thing that a Real Tween Hobo would do that would be, like, totally classic and real?" Jim was in the middle of arm-wrestling a dude named Montana Slim. They were clutching each other's hands and sweating and neither one's arm had moved in twenty-four hours. It was both boring and intense. Despite the circumstances Jim managed to mutter at me, through gritted teeth, "Steal. A. Pie."

YES!!!!! My totally awesome BFFL had saved me again. Stumptown Jim was right!!! That was exactly what I had to do to show everybody that, when it comes to being a Tween Hobo, I'm as authentic as the autographed *Twilight Saga: Breaking Dawn–Part 2* cast poster I made my mom buy me on eBay. Stealing a pie was legit! I was on it.

I ran back to the boxcar, grabbed my bindle, and headed out of Hobo Jungle into the town. Omaha is a nice little city. Unlike many other towns in our Great Midwest, it's the kind of place where you probably won't get mugged outside an off-brand fast-food BBQ establishment. Probably, you will just mosey on by, unperturbed, waving hello to the postman or a mentally ill adult on a child's bicycle. It's a classic American place, and I was on my way to do a classic American thing.

In my mind I had a rough sketch of what I was looking for: a sweet little house behind a white picket fence, a humble (and nut-free, cuz I have allergies) apple pie just cooling out on the windowsill. But I didn't seem to be in the right part of town. Instead, I found myself hiking up a big hill, flanked on either side by terrifyingly enormous mansions. Instead of picket fences, there were gates, towering gates, made of brick and steel and locked with blinking electronic sensors. All the hedges were cleanly clipped and the rosebushes smelled like new cars. Up the hill a ways I saw what looked like a gigantic gravestone, with eight lanterns stuck on top and fancy (yet boring) letters carved in gold. The letters spelled out BRENTMORE CREST. I figured some kind of toothpaste pharaoh had died here and was mummified in this lantern-encrusted tomb.

> Even before I was a hobo, I never brushed my teeth. #YOLO

I went up to investigate the tomb and was standing there just kind of stroking one of the lanterns, lost in a reverie where I was the female Paul Revere and I was riding a pony through midnight woods, barely clothed, with long strawberry-blond hair flying out behind me, strategically covering my boobs and stuff, carrying a lamp just like this one (except with an actual oil wick inside, not a fake flickering electric bulb), just warning the crap out of everybody that the British were coming. One if by land, two if by sea—and three if by unmanned telerobotic drones!

When suddenly, my peaceful war fantasy was interrupted by the loud honk of an SUV.

A mom-type lady leaned her head out and shouted at me, "Addison! Is that you? What are you doing out here? It's not safe! Does your mother know you're not in school? Why are your clothes so dirty? Here, hop in the backseat—I'll drop you off at home." Next thing I knew this lady was buckling me in. She scrunched up her nose a bit as she fastened my seat belt. "Addison, sweetheart, you need a bath." Don't I know it, I thought to myself. Been wearin' these Tuesday underpants for three months. She got back in the driver's seat, pressed a few buttons, and we drove through the gates, which opened slowly, as if they didn't feel like it.

The lady's backseat and wayback were packed with Whole Foods grocery bags and freshly dry-cleaned women's suits in swaths of plastic. As subtly as possible, I surveyed the bags for Go-Gurts and Capri Suns. The lady drove, I kept my mouth shut and let her think I was Addison, who apparently lived in the brick behemoth at the intersection of Bayberry Court and Courtberry Vista. But just as I was jumping out of the car, my bindle got snagged on one of her dry-cleaning hangers and the contents of the bindle spilled out everywhere. My glitter glue, my acorn babies, my feather hair extensions, went flying. And of all things, the lady's eyes fell right on my knife. She looked horrified. "Addison! What in the world—?! Is that—a *weapon*?!"

I grabbed my knife. We both panicked. She reached for her huge purse and suddenly I noticed that on the passenger seat beside her was a large, pristine-white box tied with ribbon. On the box a sticker said, "The Pie Factory: Genuine Homemade Pies—Apple Saffron." PIE?!?!?!?! PIE. PIE!!!!!! THERE WAS PIE IN THAT BOX.

I'm not going to specifically say what happened next.

Let's just say I stole the pie. And no one got hurt (not seriously, anyway). But I have a hunch it'll be a while before that lady speaks to Addison's parents again.

With the pie in one hand and my ragged bindle in the other, and the knife clenched in my teeth, I hightailed it out of MansionVille and ran all the way back down to Hobo Jungle. Where I was greeted with much fanfare and adoration. Stumptown Jim, who had finally, and victoriously, settled his arm-wrestling match, clapped me on the back like, you did it, kid. Tin Cap Earl, cramming pie into his face, went around getting all up in people's grills like, how you gonna say my girl Tween Hobo's a fake, yo. I regaled the guys with my violent tale and shared my pie with everybody. I didn't get enough to feel quite full, but I felt full of something else. Friendship. Bravery. Self-respect. I still didn't know who had written the insult about me (Toothpick Frank is illiterate, or that would have been a no-brainer), but I no longer cared. I knew I was just about as real as a Tween Hobo gets these days.

And that night, at the campfire, I burned the Burn Book.

MORE LIKE LAURA INGALLS
GONE WILDER

Fact: *Little House on the Prairie* is secretly gross and I can prove it. These are actual lines from the book. Rated M for Mature!

- "She had a naughty wish . . . to be bare naked . . . riding one of those gay little ponies." What?!?!
- "The tiny dickie-birds were everywhere." Are you *joking*?!
- "'Oh, Charles!' Ma said. 'You scalawag!'" Charles = Pa. They are parents. Who are *into each other.*
- "I want a papoose." Gross!
- "'Oh, I got myself a plow,' said Pa. 'Warm weather'll be here soon now, and I'll be plowing.'"

Try Laura Ingalls Wildest!!!! This book is *not* PG.

Tween Hobo @TweenHobo   4/11
Don't believe the hype—widows are not that easy to fool.

....

Tween Hobo @TweenHobo   4/12
Just bluffed a little lady in Sioux Falls outta some sweet-ass geodes.

....

Tween Hobo @TweenHobo   4/15
This actually is my first rodeo.

....

Tween Hobo @TweenHobo   4/16
As legend has it, jeans used to not be skinny.

....

Tween Hobo @TweenHobo   4/17
They say the best revenge is living well, but how about poisoning
a well?

....

Tween Hobo @TweenHobo   4/18
That thing where a bunch of hobos do a flash mob.

....

Tween Hobo @TweenHobo   4/19
My other flask is a Capri Sun.

Tween Hobo @TweenHobo   4/20

C.R.E.A.M. Cattle Roam Everywhere Around Me

....

Tween Hobo @TweenHobo   4/21

Reaping the bitter harvest of some poor FarmVille decisions

....

Tween Hobo @TweenHobo   4/22

A good Easter egg hunt should have the feel of a mini-gold rush.

....

Tween Hobo @TweenHobo   4/23

Teach me how to buggy, teach me teach me how to buggy.

The only people for me are the mad ones, the ones who are mad to live, mad to talk, mad to do Mad Libs.

⇒ HOBO ACTIVITIES ⇐

Hardscrabble traveler like me finds plenty of ways to pass the time as I do my wandering. Here are some of my favorite rainy-day hobo activities:

- Old soup can + glitter pen = personalized soup can
- Rustle up some alphabet beads, make a name bracelet
- Canning and preserving fruit #ThatsMyJam
- Maple trees #IdTapThat
- Blind Man's Bluff (Don't hate the Blind Man, hate the Bluff)
- Ropemaking #DontGetItTwisted
- Draw Something is okay, but Carve Something would be better
- Rolling a hoop with a stick is the bomb dot biz
- IRL way to make a GIF: (1) carve into a birch tree; (2) blink one eye, then the other

Sometimes the other hobos have weird ideas about what's "fun." I'm surrounded by dice sharks and crapshooters and I just wanna play Uno! Or, worst case, some Muggle Quidditch.

- Nope, sorry, fellas, don't play poker—thought you said Pokémon.
- Nope, sorry, fellas, don't play pool—thought you said pool party.
- Nope, sorry, fellas, don't bet on horses—I only bet on unicorns.

When I totally run out of ideas, I consult my phone. "Siri, what are some really dandy parlor games?" Or I try to get the guys to play kissing games. (One thing's for sure—when you play Spin the Bottle with hobos, there are plenty of bottles.) But Stumptown Jim sucks at Truth or Dare—he always picks Truth. Anyway, like I said, I get by. I sure do a lot of Mad Libs (hint: always say *boobs*, even for an adjective!!). And here's what I remind myself when I'm gambling and cardsharping: you gotta know when to hold 'em, know when to fold 'em—know when to startle your opponent with a baby Pokémon who wields unexpected abilities.

But this weekend I think I'm just gonna kick back and focus on my scrimshaw.

When life wears you down, Twi-harder.

⌁ APRIL 25 ⌁

Black Hills, South Dakota

Today I saw Mount Rushmore. It was all boys.

You know, when I left home, I was more of an indoor kid. But now that I've been traveling, sleeping outside, surviving however I can, I feel sort of closer to Nature. I feel that certain times of day are just so beautiful, I can't help but feel glad to be alive. When the sun breaks over the horizon and the day begins. Or when the sun sinks down and the day darkens to a close.

Or the special hour of each day, usually around 2:00 p.m., that I spend thinking about *Twilight*.

Today I have found the perfect spot to do my thinking–a little hollow in the woods that could easily be the setting where, for the first time, Bella saw what happens to Edward when his vampire skin is exposed to sunlight.

Here is what happens: *HE SPARKLES*.

I think about this for half an hour.

Then I think about Jacob, Edward's hot-blooded werewolf rival for Bella's love. I think about how when he turns into a wolf, his jean shorts just magically disappear. I think about those vanished jean shorts. I wonder where they go.

Then I think about Bella. Bella Swan. I think about how it would feel to have a name like that. A name that basically translates to Beautiful Squared. I think about her pale, pale skin, her dark hair, her cool relationship with her dad, her red truck, her various hoodies.

Then I think about Renesmee.

My dear Pineapple Chloe (future daughter), how I shall cherish the day when I hand down to you my beloved *Twilight* books (and DVDs). I will probably make some kind of chart as well to hand down to you, which will explain the key facts of the *Twilight* universe. Together we shall look at the chart, as I say things like "You see, Pineapple, you are my daughter, just as Renesmee was Bella's. But Renesmee was a human/vampire hybrid, whereas you are human/Bieber."

I wonder which one of my future ex-boyfriends will, like Jacob, see my baby daughter and immediately imprint on her. I wonder if that will actually be kind of weird.

What I don't want to think about, what I never want to think about, what pains me to the deepest pit of my soul, is the terrible fact that in Real Life, against every law of Love and in violation of Immortal Desire, K-Stew cheated on R-Patz. Bella cheated on Edward. The sun cheated on the moon.

When I think about this, a thunderstorm rages within me. Drops of sweat fall from my forehead onto this page. I get so mad at Kristen Stewart I want to smack her and look like her and wear her jacket and press my cheek against hers. #Feelings

I conclude my *Twilight* reverie with this. Note to self: when you're old enough to date a hot vampire, do *not* take him for granted.

Time to head back to camp and see if Hot Johnny Two-Cakes sparkles in the sun.

And btw, I didn't like *The Hunger Games.*
Too realistic.

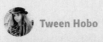 **Tween Hobo** 4/26

Might be hard for folks to call me lazy when I finish carving J-Biebz's face into the side of this mountain.

Tween Hobo @TweenHobo 4/27
Tied to the train tracks. #FML

....

Tween Hobo @TweenHobo 4/28
Oh, snap, brambles.

....

Tween Hobo @TweenHobo 4/29
Sixteen tons and what do you get, another day older and deeper in love with Justin Bieber.

Tween Hobo @TweenHobo   4/30

Ain't had a Capri Sun this tasty since I left Omaha.

....

Tween Hobo @TweenHobo   5/1

The prettiest state is South Dakota Fanning.

....

Tween Hobo @TweenHobo   5/2

Today is Stumptown Jim's birthday. I made him a gift certificate good for one companionable walk in the woods.

....

Tween Hobo @TweenHobo   5/3

The best towns are the towns that prioritize their taffy.

....

Tween Hobo @TweenHobo   5/4

Northern lights be lookin' like a screen saver.

....

Tween Hobo @TweenHobo   5/5

I learned half my Torah portion riding the rods underneath a coal car from Butte to Cheyenne.

....

Tween Hobo @TweenHobo   5/6

Any hobo dance-battle movie worth its salt had best climax in a jig-off.

....

Tween Hobo @TweenHobo   5/7

This train is bound for glory, and I am bound to get my period . . .someday.

Sometimes I feel like the only reason people hop trains is so they can post pictures of themselves doing it on Facebook.

⟩ MAY 8 ⟨

Cheyenne, Wyoming

Yesterday all the fellas caught the 3:15 to Reno and I couldn't run fast enough to catch on—so now I got a bad case a' hobo FOMO.

FOMO means Fear Of Missing Out. It's pretty hard not to feel some FOMO when you're stranded in the midst of endless prairie, lonely as sin, and all your homeys are lounging on the top deck of a train together, eating blueberries with their filthy fingers and instagramming the bejesus out of themselves.

Oh, and then you remember that your fifth-grade class got a tiny turtle whose head is even smaller than a strawberry and you haven't even gotten to imprint on him yet.

Man, Toothpick Frank is the worst. He keeps "liking" every one of Stumptown Jim's pictures, and writing little inside-jokey comments under them, like "LOL—we skinned that rat" or "Dude, where's my hooch?!" He's obviously *trying* to make me feel left out!!

Oh, no, he *di-int*. I just refreshed Facebook and now I see that Toothpick Frank has gone ahead and *replaced his profile pic with a picture of him and Stumptown Jim.*

They have their arms around each other and they're joyously carousing! Oh, that's *enough*. This is some straight-up treachery. And Stumptown Jim just *liked* it?!?!!?

Well. Two can play at this game.

Hello, Mr. Scarecrow. Ready to pose for a bunch of pictures where it looks like you and I are having the time of our lives? Cool, I thought you'd be down. Okay—let's do one where we're high-fiving. And one where we're both wearing ironic T-shirts and pointing to ourselves like, *Whaaaaa?!* And then let's take one where we're not smiling, but looking pensively out of the frame, as the sunlight hits us and it's like the viewer is getting one little glimpse of the crazy-deep adventure that is our lives.

What's this? A comment from Stumptown Jim? "Cool pic. Miss u." Oh, I bet you do. And I bet you're just frantically googling this scarecrow right now, like, who is this guy? Do I know him? Should I? And meanwhile, I'm not responding to your comment—I'm just posting a status update: *Laughing so hard it hurts.*

Who's got FOMO now, you ruthless bastards.

Tween Hobo @TweenHobo   5/9

He's Just Not That Pinto Bean

Tween Hobo @TweenHobo   5/10

Is America READY for this dandelion chain???

Tween Hobo @TweenHobo   5/11

Lord, I got the password-protected wireless-network blues . . .

Tween Hobo @TweenHobo   5/12

I got Catfished today. Big fella. Whiskers.

Tween Hobo @TweenHobo   5/13

Just helped Toothpick Frank set up his Pinterest account; his main interests are whores and carousing.

Tween Hobo @TweenHobo   5/14

If I ever find a phantom tollbooth, I'm stealing all the phantom change.

Tween Hobo @TweenHobo   5/15

This *Farmers' Almanac* is useless, it doesn't even explain how to unlock bonus crops.

Tween Hobo @TweenHobo   5/16

Justin Bieber's tweets are so random, and handsome, and brave.

Tween Hobo @TweenHobo   5/17

Balloons on a mailbox mean some little kid is about to experience a bona fide Tween Hobo cake heist.

Tween Hobo @TweenHobo　　　　　　　　　　5/18

No one ever lies on their deathbed and says, "I wish I hadn't collected so many dreamcatchers."

....

Tween Hobo @TweenHobo　　　　　　　　　　5/19

My Traveling Pants are starting to smell weird.

 **Tween Hobo**

I feel sorry for them hobos who never knew a mother's love—cuz my mom once signed me up for a make-your-own-plate class.

COOL THINGS ABOUT MY BROTHER, WHEREVER I MAY FIND HIM

He is almost seventeen.

He got his driver's license, and then he got it revoked.

He wears headphones 99 percent of the time.

He's good at every video game ever invented.

He writes on his bedroom ceiling in permanent marker.

He has a poster on his wall of a kitten in midair with flames shooting out of its butt that says, "I Must Go—My Planet Needs Me."

He's the one who came up with naming our wireless network Bill Wi the Science Fi.

He wears stupid T-shirts on purpose.

He is mean to me in front of his new friends.

He secretly loves me.

Vaudeville killed the pantomime star.

⋛ MAY 21 ⋚

Boise, Idaho

Something you might not know about me is that I can really sing. I know it sounds conceited, and I wouldn't even mention it except that I am truly, like, *wildly* good at singing. The only thing I'm better at than singing is stuffing grapes into my cheeks and then smashing my fists against the bulges so I get fifty squirts of grape juice shooting through my teeth at once. When I sing, the joy and light that goes flooding out of me is so intense I'm like, um, how come bluebirds aren't doing my hair right now? Not only do I sing, I also rap. For instance:

It's the remix to ignition
Tween Hobo edition
I got a nut allergy
Just ask my pediatrician

My talent is a gift that I thank myself for every day.

Out on the road, there ain't much in the way of entertainment. (Even my YouTube playlists have gone stale.) So we do a lot of gathering and banjo-picking and open-air crunking. Stumptown Jim's got his old guitar, Hot Johnny Two-Cakes has his harmonica (which he often just kind of kisses, to show off his lips), and I've got what Shakira would refer to as "the Voice." We do old hillbilly classics, traveling songs, spirituals—and I try to put a new-style spin on the old gems:

St. Peter, don't you call me cuz I can't go
I owe my soul to Forever 21.

Or:

Come gather, Beliebers, wherever you roam
Oh, his voice, it is a-changin' . . .

And, of course, that old chestnut "I Ain't Gonna Work on Maggie's FarmVille No More." (Maggie, if you're reading this, STOP SENDING ME FARMVILLE REQUESTS!!!!)

I also try to teach the guys some of the latest hits, putting them in words they'll understand:

Hopped off the train in Idaho with a dream and my cardigan
Noddin' my head like "yeah"
Playin' my spoons like "whoa"

And:

Hey! I just met you
And this is crazy!
But here's a tin can
So call me, maybe!

We have a real good time. Or at least—we *used* to. Until this week. When everything went wrong.

The trouble began on Monday morning, in a vacant lot near the Boise Amtrak station. Stumptown Jim was tearing off strips of newspaper to start a trash-can fire. I was standing behind him on an upside-down plastic milk crate, trying to fishtail-braid his hair, when suddenly, an advertisement in the newspaper caught my eye: "Is YOUR CHILD a STAR???" Then, below that: "Could YOUR CHILD make a MUSIC VIDEO that would get ONE MILLION HITS???". And then there was this grainy, newspapery photo collage of a proud white mother, a bulky computer, a cartoon keyboard, and a chubby, curly-haired, blond girl in a leotard flanked by three other children of assorted nonwhite races with her hands on her hips like, *I did it.*

Eagerly I scanned these images and synthesized their meaning. "Stumptown Jim!" I cried. "There's some kind of off-brand Ark Music Factory–type joint in this town, making professional-quality digital videos for underage amateurs! I could be the next Rebecca Black! And all we have to do is raise"—I grabbed the paper and checked the fine print—"dang. Two thousand bucks?!!" I clutched the paper to my chest and wailed a timeless lament: "This suuuuuuuuuucccckkkkkksssss!!!!!!!!!"

Well, if there's one thing Stumptown Jim's good at, it's being hopeless, so we got right down to it. He busted out his old guitar and strummed and stared off into the great unforgiving yonder, while I wept and wiped my eyes and wept again. As the trash-can fire crackled, I sang low, sad songs—songs like *I am a tween / Of constant sorrow.* I sang, and Jim played, and the fire smoked, and there we were—at rock bottom.

But you know me—I'm irrepressible. Plus, YOLO, etc. So I didn't stay down for long. I popped right back up like a bath toy, and I go, Jim! Wait a darn sec. I don't need these fancy producers. It's the twenty-first century and we're in the United States of America!!!! I have GarageBand, iMovie, YouTube, two thumbs, a magical singing voice—and a buttload of moxie. I am my own producer!!! Jim, don'tcha see? I can do it myself! I can go it alone! I CAN BECOME . . . A MEME.

By this point I was twerking so hard that all the trash cans in the area were vibrating and my loose tooth fell out. Jim's eyes were full of prairie. But I think he caught my drift. So we packed up our spoons and went to shoot a "Call Me Maybe" parody video in a graveyard.

———————

The next day was Tuesday. Happens to be a lucky day for me, because it's the only day of the week when the day-of-the-week underpants I was wearing when I left home are factually correct. Jim and I put the finishing touches on our video (couple hyperlinks; a black screen at the end with a note in some supersquiggly font [which Jim called cursive, which, huh?!—never heard of it] that said, *In Memoriam: Floyd Caboose* [he died while making the video, RIP]). I uploaded it to my YouTube channel and we crossed all our remaining fingers.

As we waited for the views and likes to start racking up, Jim and I split a can of beans and I hummed some Rebecca Black, as if to mystically summon the powers of the internet. *Yesterday was Thursday* . . . eats beans . . . *Today it is Friday* . . . licks spoon . . . *We, we, we, so excited* . . . more beans . . .

Nothing. Not a single view (aside from the lousy three that Jim and I had given ourselves). I refreshed and refreshed and refreshed. It was hopeless! No one was watching our video. We were broke and lonely and unfamous. All we had was each other, which, barf. And somehow, Jim didn't even care. He kept saying all this junk about how to him, making the video in the graveyard was an *experience*, and it was the *experience* that mattered, in the end. I was like, Jim, don't you *realize* that *nothing matters* unless *other people like it*?!?! I started to think maybe I had picked the wrong hobo to help me go viral.

Just then, Tin Cap Earl wandered over to us. He was wearing a neon-yellow mesh tank top and singing Lady Gaga. "I'm beautiful in my way, 'cause God makes no mistakes, I'm on the *TRAIN TRACKS BABY*, I was born this way!" Something told me Tin Cap Earl could help.

Sure enough, he had lots of advice: "You gotta sex it up. What gets hits on the internet? Animals. Korean songs. And sexy stuff. Put yourself in one, ideally two, of those categories. You'll blow up like the World Trade."

Jim goes, "Too soon."

Tin Cap Earl, fresh as ever, goes, "Too *spoon*." And played the spoons for a second, banging them sassily against his hip.

Meanwhile I had already taken his words to heart. I yanked my ponytail way over to the side, threw on my heart-shaped sunglasses, tied my T-shirt up so my whole midriff was exposed, and wiped glittery lotion all over my stomach. I looked almost illegally hot. I was like, let's go, Jim, let's reshoot the thing.

But Jim wouldn't hear of it. He went off on a classic Stumptown Jim–style rant. He goes, "I hate a song that makes you think that you're not any good. I hate a song that makes you think you're just born to lose. Bound to lose. No good to nobody. No good for nothing. Because you're too old or too young or too fat or too slim or too ugly or too this or that. Songs that run you down or poke fun at you on account of your bad luck or hard traveling. I am out to fight those songs to my very last breath of air and my last drop of blood!" And he lifts his guitar way up in the air and goes, "THIS MACHINE KILLS FASCISTS!!"*

But I only heard that part from a distance, cuz me and Tin Cap were already halfway down the road, planning out our first shot: me in a bikini, standing over the camera sucking a Blow Pop.

By Wednesday, the new video was up on YouTube, Facebook, Tumblr, and Twitter. The comments were rolling in. Unfortunately, they were not quite what I'd expected. Most of them seemed to be written by members of the Taliban? Or maybe some of the mean girls at my school? They said things like "U r so lame it makes me want to kill myself" or, coming from a different perspective, "U suck so bad please kill yourself." By the time I'd scrolled through a hundred of these, I was pretty much a cutter. Tin Cap Earl kept saying, "It's avant-garde, they just don't get it, it's way over their heads," but that was not comforting to me. I wanted my Voice to Touch the People. I wanted to Heal What Was Broken in This Land. I wanted my Video to Get One Million Hits. I didn't want to be humiliated.

Yesterday was Thursday. Today it is Friday. Friday. Everybody's looking forward to the weekend. Weekend.

Around the campfire tonight, Jim took out his old guitar and started to strum. "Why don't you sing something for us," he

---

* According to Google, someone named Woody Guthrie really said all that, and Stumptown Jim was biting his style.

asked me. But I just hung my head and sighed. My singing days are behind me now, I said. The people have spoken and what they said was, I suck. I'll never be famous now, I said. I'll never go viral.

Jim looked at me funny. "Well, now, you didn't come all this way just to get famous, did you? I thought you had something more important on your mind. Something to do with searching out the truth. Something to do with locating your brother."

I stared into the fire. For some reason, it floated back into my mind, that phrase my brother wrote on his bedroom ceiling. "Life is pointless." Was he right? All I knew was I missed him now more than ever.

"Yeah," I said gloomily. "But it's hopeless. I'll never track him down. All I know is that he went to something called 'rehab' somewhere in California. That's not much info to go on. No, let's face it, Jim. I'll probably never see my brother, Evan, again."

To my surprise, Hot Johnny Two-Cakes suddenly perked up and addressed me directly for the first time in recorded history: "What's this? You got a brother named Evan who went to rehab?"

Startled by his interest, and eager to seem like I wasn't internally pulling off a 540 McTwist on my emotional skateboard because he'd spoken to me, I responded curtly, "What's it to you?"

"I think I know that kid," Hot Johnny replied, cool as a jumbo freezie.

"What do you mean, you *know* him? Where do you know him from?"

"Met him on Second Life," said Hot Johnny, matter-of-fact.

While my mind reeled, Stumptown Jim asked for clarification. "Second Life? Jumping Jehoshaphat. What in the name of holy creation is *that*?"

Toothpick Frank jumped in. "You never heard'a Second Life?" he jeered. "You been out on the rails too long, buddy. You need to check in with civilization again." (A little aggressive for a dude who just the other day found out about Pinterest, I thought, but whatever.)

"It's an online virtual world," said Hot Johnny, yawning. "Been around since the early oughts. Used to be kind of fun, now it sucks. But this band I like did a virtual record-signing at this virtual music store. And that kid Evan was there. I remember him, cuz his avatar was the Kool-Aid Man. He kept, like, busting through walls and whatever. It was pretty tight."

I was in total shock. First of all, this was the most words I had ever heard Hot Johnny say, at least all at once. And second, I knew he was right. My brother loves the Kool-Aid Man. He has him on a T-shirt and everything. Plus, he's *always* online playing weird games and hanging around digital e-commerce locations like that. It had to be him.

Hot Johnny kept on, "Yeah, Evan. Kid was a trip. Told me all about how his parents were sending him to this treatment place, spending all kinds of cash, telling him that he had to clean up his act. He used to laugh about it. Said he was getting an all-expenses-paid vacation."

Now I was getting superexcited. "That sounds just like him!" I clapped. "That's my brother! Oh, Hot Johnny Two-Cakes, you magnificent hipster! Tell me—*do you know where he is?!?!*"

"I'm not a hipster," said Hot Johnny, and I could feel him growing cold toward me again. Tin Cap Earl snorted rather obviously at this. Hot Johnny, ignoring him, went on, "And, no, I don't know the name of the place." Hot Johnny yawned again. "But he said he was going to LA."

"Los Angeles!" I cried. "City of Angels! Okay! Well, that makes things easy, doesn't it?! There can't be too many of these 'rehabs' in LA!"

Hot Johnny seemed to have drifted off into sleep. But Tin Cap Earl and Stumptown Jim were joyful. "See now!" said Jim. "Just when you think things are hopeless, you catch a lucky break. We'll be in Los Angeles before too long. And we'll track your brother down when we get there."

"Oh, HECK YES, we will!" I cheered.

"Now then," said Jim. And the firelight danced. "Now you got to sing. But you got to do it for the right reasons. For joy. Not for a spectacle. You sing for the song itself, because that song just needs to be sung. And it's burstin' out of you. And because no matter how rough or low-down you feel, singin' will lift you up again. Now come on. Let's sing something."

I took a deep breath. I felt my veins growing warmer. Jim strummed his guitar. And I opened my mouth and sang!

"And I was like, baby, baby, baby, ooh! Like, baby, baby, baby, oh! Thought you'd always be mine, mine . . ."

On the second chorus, the rest of the guys joined in. Well, except for Toothpick Frank. He just laughed a nasty laugh. Or possibly it was a cough. He's sick as a dog and so are Salt Chunk Annie and Blind Hank and Whiskey Bob. Looks like this ague's gone viral :(

LA OR BUST!!!!!!!!!!!

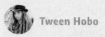 **Tween Hobo**

If I had a hammer / I'd put stickers on it.

FALCON

I will now present my research on an important subject: the subject of Me getting a Pet Falcon.

This research has been extensive. My Gmail threads are all like Re: Re: Fwd: Fwd: Fwd: FALCON.

Question: If I have ADD, then how am I so focused on getting a pet falcon?

Second question: What should I name my pet falcon? I'm thinking either Oberon or Jazzy.

Fact: Having a pet falcon can be dangerous, because suddenly you don't care about anything besides the falcon.

Okay—not saying I'll give up falconry if the answer's no, but do they have fingerless gauntlets?

Falcon biz got old. Guess I'll strap this tiny hood to a corn-husk doll, shove her in the cockpit of an old model plane, and call it a day.

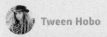 **Tween Hobo**

YOLO (You Only Log Once)

Tween Hobo @TweenHobo   5/25
Is there some kind of app I can download to spot nearby circuses?

Tween Hobo @TweenHobo   5/26
Another bunch'a rotten luck: jumpin' the night train outta Spo-
kane I lost like eighteen of my origami swans.

Tween Hobo @TweenHobo   5/27
Worked a whole day for some black-eyed peas—cuz I thought
the man was talking about the *band.* #FML

Tween Hobo @TweenHobo   5/28
Ragamuffins don't come gluten-free.

Tween Hobo @TweenHobo   5/29
Whittlin' (on Ritalin).

Tween Hobo @TweenHobo   5/30

I ain't sayin' she's a gold digger—but she *is* panning for gold in the Yukon Territory.

Tween Hobo @TweenHobo   5/31

Today we cross the border into a Chipotle.

Tween Hobo @TweenHobo   6/1

Cain't sleep a wink, bedroll's too thin, plus Hot Johnny Two-Cakes won't text me back :(

Tween Hobo @TweenHobo   6/2

The video game of my life would be *Grand Theft Scrunchie*.

Tween Hobo @TweenHobo   6/3

Holla at me if you've been to town and learned all the new dances.

Tween Hobo @TweenHobo   6/4

My teepee has heart stencils.

HISTORY'S GREATEST TWEETS

Doing a report on History's Greatest Tweets.

1. "TGIC!! (Thank God It's Canada)"—Harriet Tubman @tubster
2. "HEADS UP GUYZ THE BRITISH R COMInGg"
   —@PaulyDingDong
3. "Women should TOTES have the right to VOTE"—Susan B. Anthony @CoinsAreDollarsToo
4. "We're related to monkeys. #DealWithIt"—@Darwinning
5. "@lewis @clark Been by this ocean 15 mins where u at" —Sacajawea @NotPocahontas
6. "Check out this link for one weird old trick about #corngrowing (h/t @NausetPeople)"—@pilgrimdude1
7. "We hold these truths to be self-evident: that Taco Bell's new Monterey Jack chicken burrito is flavortastic." —@ThomasJeff / (Promoted Tweet)
8. "Shocker: I flew a kite today and it got #real. Click over to my blog for more info"—Ben Franklin @PhillyLove
9. "If I drown, I'm not a witch. If I float, you'll kill me anyway. #Mondays"—@GoodySalem
10. "Sorry, brah, it's all in the game RT @Caesar Et tu Brute?"—@BrutusXLIV

⋛ JUNE 6 ⋚

Salt Lake City, Utah

If life on the road has taught me one thing, it's that you never know what's coming next. We're on our way to LA to find my brother, but things have gotten even more exciting. I *knew* I was destined to meet Stumptown Jim, but until tonight I didn't exactly know why. Well, you're not going to believe this. Stumptown Jim, it turns out, has a brother too. A missing brother. OMG, I don't want to spoil it for you! Just gather round and let me blow your mind.

So, it was a typical night down in Hobo Jungle. Campfire. Harmonicas. A few bad women. Me and Tin Cap Earl were doing our Dr Pepper hand-slap routine and sharing the edible parts of a (spoiled alert) rotten head of cabbage. Blind Hank was inexpertly gutting a fish, Toothpick Frank was futzing with his Pinterest page, and a couple other guys just lay there slowly dying.

Stumptown Jim seemed to be in a foul mood. The light in his eyes had gone dim, and he kept letting out this low, sad whistle. At a certain point I was like, "What is the *deal* with Stumptown Jim tonight?" Tin Cap shook his head. "He gets like this sometimes. When the past creeps up on him, he gets lost in it." I was like, "Yeah, *okay*, but he doesn't have to be such a Debbie Downer." I purposely said this loud enough for Jim to overhear. But he continued to look hollow and ignore me.

Whiskey Bob, overhearing us, chimed in, "Betcha six Buffalo nickels he's thinkin' back on the day he got the name Stumptown Jim. You ever hear the story of why they call him that?" Um, *no*, I said. Tell me now. "It's not my place to tell," said Whiskey Bob. "You'll have to ask him yourself. And if I were you, I wouldn't ask right now." But you're not me, I said. If you were, you'd be much more well versed in the works of Judy Blume. And I'm not gonna sit here and let my BFFL *blubber* all night. I went right up to Stumptown Jim and flicked him on the ear.

"Dude," I said. "What is your malfunction?" Fast-forward through twelve minutes of sorrowful silence. Then, finally: "The past," he said. "The past is gone. Gone and lost and vanished and ain't never comin' back." Okay, yeah, duh, I said. But we're here right now, aren't we? Can't we just chillax? "Part of me's here," he said. "And part of me ain't."

"Stop speaking in riddles," I told him. "Riddles are for math books and long car rides. What happened to you in the past? What's the secret reason why they call you Stumptown Jim?"

A giant gasp was heard around the campsite. Multiple hobos gasping at once is a truly hideous sound. Like some kind of sewer being dredged. Plus, with that ague still going around, there was extra phlegm. I refused to be swayed: "Out with it, buddy, Best friends don't keep secrets from each other."

Jim bowed his head so low he was practically underground. Then, all at once, he straightened up, and with the courage of a Powerpuff Girl, he told his story.

The Story of Why They Call Him Stumptown Jim

Kid (this is Stumptown Jim talking now), before you were born, there was a music festival. It was called Woodstock '99.

Folks traveled from all across the land to join hands and sing along to the powerful tunes of bands like Guster, Korn, and the String Cheese Incident. It was meant to be a positive gathering, a communal celebration of light and love and the human spirit, with single-serving pizzas available for $12 and bottled water available for $4. But the gods did not smile upon the weekend. And things went dreadfully wrong.

My younger brother and I had journeyed to the festival together, hoping to barter for food and friends with some rad wallets we had made out of duct tape. My brother, who was really quite young at the time, was jittery, nervous, and wild. It was to be his first concert—and what a lineup! What a show! G. Love and Special Sauce were there. Everclear was there. Rusted Root. The Offspring. Jamiroquai.

And best of all, on Saturday night, we would stand in the presence of, and be rocked by, the magnificence known as Limp Bizkit. Limp! What a word to call such hard men! We laughed at the irony. "This will be a night to remember!" exclaimed my little bro, tossing the last of our duct-tape wallets into the air. And how right he was. But the memory is a harrowing one.

Only a few songs into their set, maestro Fred Durst and the Bizkit ensemble dove into a stirring rendition of their hit single "Break Stuff." And the crowd, a horde of maniacs in checkerboard Vans, took the chorus all too literally. Break stuff they did, as if Dionysus himself had arisen in the soul-patched, Kangol-hatted face of Durst and commanded them to destroy the very ritual of music itself. They tore plywood from the walls, overturned the Porta Potties, set plastic bottles on fire. The mosh pit became a serpents' den. And my little brother was caught in the mix!

I was momentarily blinded due to somebody's breaking a glow stick and splooging its phosphorescent liquid in my eyes. When my vision cleared, I had lost sight of my brother. I called out for him, panicked, and began to force my way through the mob. Up on the stage, Fred Durst was halfheartedly advocating against further violence, while at the same time making it known that he did not want us to "mellow out" like some risible Alanis Morissette listeners. At the very mention of Morissette's name I saw a girl get punched in the face. Where was my brother?! I scanned the flickering darkness.

At last I spotted him—and not a moment too soon. Hidden behind some enormous speakers, he was up against a wall, held hostage by a quartet of Juggalos. Yes, Juggalos—those devoted worshippers of the Insane Clown Posse, who channel their aggression against more commercial music acts into black-and-white face paint, twisted Caucasian dreadlocks, and a tongue-in-cheek attitude toward basic hygiene. These Juggalos had captured my little brother, who had made the rookie mistake of wearing a Limp Bizkit T-shirt to a Limp Bizkit concert and had thus inspired their condescending rage. "You think this nonsense is authentic?!" one of them spat at him. "This ain't real! This ain't underground! Them jokers is just MTV's copy of ICP!" My brother stammered, and tears sprang to his eyes, possibly from fear, but more likely from sheer disappointment.

I tapped the biggest Juggalo on the shoulder. "Say, fellas," I began, hoping to reason with them. All four whipped around, their painted faces more open than I expected. We might have all become friends were it not for the unfortunate puncturing of our little moment by a hot-pink explosion. A gang of paintball warriors had come blasting through the crowd, fully decked out in kneepads and face masks. They wielded their Crayola-spurting weaponry like trained soldiers, and despite an evident shared interest in *paint*, it seemed their enemy number one was any and all Insane Clowns. A messy, neon-tinted battle erupted, as the fires burned in the distance and Durst licked his microphone.

I was fending off a Juggalo with one arm and kicking away a paintball gun with one leg when I saw that my brother was about to be shot, at close range. With all the fraternal love in the world I leapt to save him. As I dove in front of him, making myself into his human shield, the trigger was pulled. I got shot. Right in the crotch. I felt like my soul was on fire. Later, at the emergency room, the doctors shook their heads. There was nothing they could do. My physical being had been abruptly deformed. In short, they broke my junk. Those paintball guns should really come with warnings, the doctors said.

My brother felt so guilty, and I so ashamed, that we never spoke of what happened. Shortly thereafter I left home, catching out on my first train ride. I haven't seen my brother in over a decade. If he thinks of me still, he thinks of me as "Jim." The Jim I used to be. Whereas out here, on the road, everybody knows me as the man I now am. The man with only a useless stump. Stumptown Jim.

Okay—WHOA. That was intense! And semi-inappropriate! But he's done talking now. It's me again. Tween Hobo. #Represent

Finished with his story, Jim sat by the fire, worn-out. The other hobos held their heads in their hands and moaned. I tried to come up with an adequate response. "Uh, *YIKES*," I said. "That *suuuuccckkkssss*."

"You're tellin' me," sighed Jim.

"The saddest part," I said, "is that you never saw your brother again. Don't you miss him?"

"I'm not sure that's the saddest part. But, yeah, I do. I kinda get to wonderin' what he's up to, now and again."

Okay—now here's where the amazeballs part occurs. When Jim said, "Now and again," he glanced down at his left wrist. His *left wrist.* Where, I noticed for the first time, *he was wearing a bracelet. A weird old leather-string bracelet.* A BRACELET EXACTLY THE SAME AS MR. BRINK'S!!!!!!?!?!?!?!?!?!?!!!!!!?!?!??!!?!?!!!!

If I'd been an owl, my head would have spun all the way around. If I'd had a pet falcon, I would have launched it into the heavens with the command, "Jazzy! Fly! Fly back to Charlottesville and tell Mr. Brink that *I have found his missing brother*!!!!!"

110

Since no birds of prey were available, I basically just gawked. Jim was like, "What?" And I was like, "Brace . . . let . . ." He goes, "This old thing? What about it?"

I was about to start gushing and yodeling all over Hobo Jungle about how Jim and Mr. Brink were long-lost brothers and how thanks to yours truly Tween Hobo they could now be reunited, but I saw this strange little twitch in Jim's eye, and it stopped me. I knew my BFFL pretty well at this point, and something told me he wasn't ready to see his brother again. All in good time, I told myself. And now I had a powerful secret.

"What about it?" Jim asked again.

I drummed up a reply. "Oh—nothing. It just reminds me of—well. It reminds me of *my* brother. And how much I miss him. Oh, Jim, do you think I'll ever see my brother again?!"

"Of course I do. We're going out to LA to find him, ain't we?"

"Yeah," I said, staring at the fire. "I hope so." And I bit my lip to stop myself from grinning.

(Btw, sometimes I wish I'd lived through historic times, but that Woodstock '99 sounds like a real nightmare.)

Tween Hobo @TweenHobo   6/7

To stay safe on the rails I have to look like a boy, but that's okay, because Justin Bieber looks like a girl.

....

Tween Hobo @TweenHobo   6/8

I'm so hungry I could eat a Trivial Pursuit pie with all six wedges filled in.

Tween Hobo @TweenHobo 6/9

Give a man a fish, he'll eat for a day. Give a man a hypercolor T-shirt, he'll look awesome for the rest of his life.

....

Tween Hobo @TweenHobo 6/10

Unlike most kids my age, I have like a one-fortnight attention span.

....

Tween Hobo @TweenHobo 6/11

The problem with middle school boys is they don't have huge beards.

....

Tween Hobo @TweenHobo 6/12

With all my creativity and spunk I'll definitely get a good job someday. Or at least a good . . . cardboard box.

....

Tween Hobo @TweenHobo 6/13

Someday they'll tell my story on a really notorious Wikipedia page.

....

Tween Hobo @TweenHobo 6/14

Might you allow a poor beggar past the mesh gates to your bouncy castle?

....

Tween Hobo @TweenHobo 6/15

I'm just a low-down, rascally scamp, but the elegance of a tube-to-mouth yogurt-delivery system is not lost on me.

....

Tween Hobo @TweenHobo 6/16

My folks never larned me no netiquette.

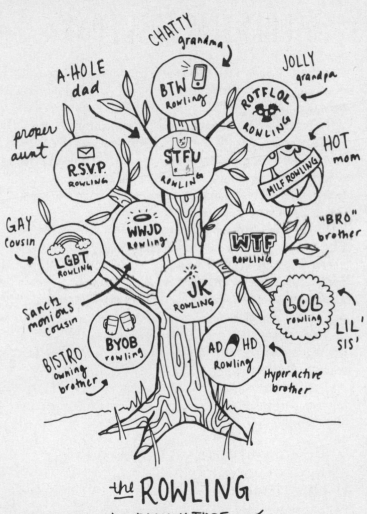

CHATTY grandma

JOLLY grandpa

A·HOLE dad

proper aunt

HOT mom

GAY cousin

"BRO" brother

Sanctimonious cousin

LIL' SIS'

BISTRO owning brother

Hyperactive brother

BTW Rowling

ROTFLOL ROWLING

R.S.V.P. ROWLING

STFU ROWLING

MILF ROWLING

WWJD Rowling

WTF ROWLING

LGBT ROWLING

JK ROWLING

LOL rowling

BYOB rowling

AD HD Rowling

the ROWLING
→ FAMILY TREE ←

⇥ SUBTWEETS TO A PONY ⇤

Subtweet (noun): a tweet posted with the specific intention of getting a message across subliminally to someone who you hope will be reading it.

Example: A boy with a crush on his camp counselor, the one who was always down at the waterfront handling the canoes, might tweet: "Got canoeing on my mind . . ."

Then, when the camp counselor, who follows him, sees the tweet, she might realize that he has *her* on his mind. This would make it an effective subtweet.

Of course the problem with subtweets is that you never know who's reading your tweets and mistakenly assuming your subtweets are directed at them. So, for example, when this kid tweets, "Got canoeing on my mind . . . ," he might be horrified to realize that the tweet has been seen by the girl in Bunk 6 who stalked him all summer and *she* thinks he's referring to the time she was stern and he was bow and they rowed all the way to the creepy island in the middle of the lake. And now she thinks he likes her back.

So to avoid having a situation like that on my hands, I'm just gonna come out and say exactly who these subtweets are meant for.

These are my SUBTWEETS TO A PONY:

Tween Hobo @TweenHobo   6/18
Fantasizing about feeding oats to a certain someone.
#SubtweetToAPony

Tween Hobo @TweenHobo   6/18

There's someone out there who I think is top-notch. He has a
black spot on his nose. I'm not saying his name tho.
#SubtweetToAPony

....

Tween Hobo @TweenHobo   6/18

You think you're great because your nose is so soft, like I even
care. #SubtweetToAPony

....

Tween Hobo @TweenHobo   6/18

I want a #PONY2012. #SubtweetToAPony

....

Tween Hobo @TweenHobo   6/18

Wild horses couldn't drag me back home but a pony?—yeah, that
could. #SubtweetToAPony

A FACEBOOK MESSAGE FROM THE FIFTH-GRADER FORMERLY KNOWN AS TESSA, MY SECOND-BEST FRIEND

Today I got a Facebook message from Tessa!!!! Copied here in its full pain-in-the-buttness.

> Wednesday, 7:48 p.m.
> **From: Tessa Alexandra**
>
> umm . . . where are u . . . lol?! we finished 5th grade wit out u :(now it's summer vacay—r u ever coming back to c-ville??? u missed a lot at skool this year—we got a lil turtle—he's soooooooooo cute but he still doesn't have a name :(. we also had to memorize some "great american poems." it was booooorrrinnnggg so i just did ke$ha lyrics instead :) oh, but guess what?! mr. brink got switched from 5th to 6th so he's gonna b our teacher again next yr!!!!! also kevin r. is still #gross. he eats too many #cheetos. im rly sad becuz u r my 2nd-bffl and u r missing :(. i dont want to hurt ur feelvings but if u dont come back soon i might make Emma 2nd and u 3rd.
> pls come back soon cutie pieeeee.
> miss u
>
> xoooxoxoxoxooxox
> mrs. tessa jonas

Tween Hobo @TweenHobo   6/19

This railroad cop's telling me how I need to buy a valid ticket and I'm all *looks straight into camera*.

....

Tween Hobo @TweenHobo   6/20

Rainbows remind me there is always hope I might get to eat some Lucky Charms.

....

Tween Hobo @TweenHobo   6/21

Most of the traveling salesmen I meet are selling illegal DVDs.

....

Tween Hobo @TweenHobo   6/22

This ham radio I built started playing NPR and I freaked out cuz I thought my parents had found me.

....

Tween Hobo @TweenHobo   6/23

The life of a drifter is like having recess 24/7. But without good snacks.

Tween Hobo @TweenHobo   6/24
If you are what you eat, then I am the world's dingiest Tootsie Roll.

....

Tween Hobo @TweenHobo   6/25
Lesson learned. You can't buy cupcakes with Monopoly money.

....

Tween Hobo @TweenHobo   6/26
Maybe Miley cut her hair and sold it to buy Liam Hemsworth a watch chain not knowing that he had sold his watch to buy her a fine scrunchie.

....

Tween Hobo @TweenHobo   6/27
I could murder a Snickers.

....

Tween Hobo @TweenHobo   6/28
If you ask me, the phrase *magic beans* is redundant.

....

Tween Hobo @TweenHobo   6/29
Opened cupboard, found Indian. #ItJustGotReal

GREAT AMERICAN POEMS

(by Tween Hobo)

The woods are lovely, dark, and deep
But I have promises to keep,
And I have to wear my stupid retainer when I sleep.

———————————

I took the road less traveled by.
And that is why I will probz have to repeat 5th grade :(

———————————

Because I could not stop for Death
I fell off a pipe and lost *Super Mario Galaxy 2* for Wii

———————————

I saw the best minds of my generation
Do just fine without Ritalin on school holidays and weekends

———————————

This is just to say
I have eaten
the plums
that were in
the icebox
And also
I drank the purple stuff

O Captain! My Captain! @RealCapnCrunch

———————————

There's a stake in your fat black heart
And the villagers never liked you
If I can't have a vampire-theme bat mitzvah
Daddy, Daddy, we're through

———————————

What happens to a dream deferred?
Does it dry up
Like a raisin in the sun?
Or does it sparkle
Like Edward Cullen in the sun?!?!!? ♡

———————————

13 going on 30 ways of looking at a blackbird

———————————

I sing the body electric
I do the electric slide

———————————

so much depends
upon
me
doing the chicken dance

SOME IMMATURE THINGS THAT HOBOS DO

When I skipped town and left fifth grade, I thought I was leaving certain kinds of foolishness behind me. But it turns out that most hobos be actin' like they in middle school. Here are some of the typically immature things that hobos do.

- Hobos be claiming they have a retainer when it's just a straightened-out paper clip.
- Hobos be talking at the same time and then they go "Jinx"!
- Hobos be trying to write *PEN 15* on my hand like that's funny.
- Hobos be calling their hair blond when it's just light brown.
- Hobos be slowly "turning up the volume" on their middle fingers.
- Hobos be like, "Your epidermis is showing."
- Hobos be like, "Stop hitting yourself," as they're slapping me with my own hand.
- Hobos be cliquey.
- Hobos be asking each other, "What's your favorite dinosaur?"
- Hobos be stressing out about cooties.
- Hobos be dating all these secret camp girlfriends in Canada.

- Hobos be pairing up for three-legged races.
- Hobos be making their calculators say *BOOBS*.
- Hobos be snapping bras.

Is the national anthem considered a slow dance?

⊰ FOURTH OF JULY ⊱

Happy birthday, America!!!!!!!! It's motherflipping INDEPEN-DENCE DAY and I'm charging through the Nevada desert on this bucking bronco of a freight train, with my T-shirt tied up so my midriff shows, wearing six pairs of sunglasses at once. Because IT'S A FREE COUNTRY, folks!!!! That means you can get your ears pierced twice on one side and once on the other! That means the government only keeps a few extra copies of all your emails! That means YOU CAN WEAR PAJAMAS TO THE MOVIES.

I tell you what—if the English actor Robert Pattinson, who portrays Edward Cullen in the *Twilight* movie franchise, were to board this train right now and offer to fly me away on a private jet to Buckingham Palace, I would straight-up decline. "Not today, Robert Pattinson," I would say. "Not today." Here's the thing about British people: they have such good manners that they thought it was proper to fight a war wearing bright red coats. Meanwhile us "rude" Americans discovered a little thing called "camouflage," hid in the trees, and beat the crap out of them. And camouflage is still trendy today. What's the moral? Eat with your hands, don't say thank you, and you'll be a global superpower for at least a few centuries until China takes over.

America looks different from a freight train. TBH it looks kind of more boring. I mean, sure, there are the majestic vistas, the amber waves of grain (#nofilter), the mountains and the trees and the rivers and the prairie. But you don't see as many advertisements. And I love advertisements. I like to know what video games are rated M for Mature and which products are now available with a hint of lime. I try to stay absolutely up-to-the-minute on which toys now come with which meals. I like to know there's a lawyer I could call one day in the far future if I was to suffer a workplace injury.

I like to think that all the happy families in the advertisements live in one insanely happy town where all the moms wear fresh khakis as they load up the backs of their SUVs and all the dads burst in after work with piping-hot buckets of fried chicken and everyone goes on affordable vacations and all the kids get everything they want.

One of my favorite things to see in an advertisement is a fake to-do list. It'll be written in perfect mom-handwriting, and maybe the golden pen the imaginary mom used to write it will be lying there, askew, atop the digitally rendered day planner. The list will say something like "Pick up Jessica at flute practice. Water plants. Talk to a State Farm insurance representative about all my options." When I see a list like that, I get a little choked up. Because the mom is taking such good care of her family. And doing it with such brisk elegance. That Jessica is a lucky girl, to have such a mother.

Speaking of moms, I got a text from my mom yesterday. It said, "Your tweets are lots of fun. Sounds like you're doing some real hands-on learning. Don't forget to take your medication." That was it. Not a word about coming home. Not a word about my brother. Total zombie text. The more I looked at it, the more I felt there was actually something kind of spooky about it.

Or no. Maybe *spooky*'s not the word. Maybe it's more like *suspicious*. Maybe this is one of my mom's psychological tricks. Like she thinks if she just plays along with this whole thing and doesn't act like it's inappropriate that I'm on a cross-country sleepover party for infinity-plus-one nights with a posse of vagrants, maybe I'll just lose interest in the whole thing and come running home to her. Like if she acts like she doesn't *care* where I am, maybe I'll just get to thinking about that one super-smushed-up corner of the couch in the TV room where, when I cuddle up in it, I feel like a baby pillow pressed up against some kind and warm adult pillows. Like I'd ever get homesick for *that*.

Well, even if I did get homesick for that—even if maybe I'm crying a little bit right now because I miss my mom *a lot*—I can't go home. Not yet. I have to find my brother. And I'm close. Another night or two and we'll be in California! Where, who knows, we might just run into Justin Bieber at a 7-Eleven or something! And then also I have to figure out some way to reunite Stumptown Jim and Mr. Brink. Jeez, *I've* got a to-do list. Fetch me my golden pen, Jessica!

Plus, who cares about TV-room couches when you're stretched out on the deck of a freight train zooming through the Nevada desert on the Fourth of July. Toothpick Frank just tossed me a mostly not rotten peach. All the tensions between us about who's BFFLs and stuff have melted away in the summer sun. We've settled everything, and the upshot is we're all going to be buddies for life. I can't exactly put my finger on it, but the farther we ride, the more I'm starting to get the feeling I know What Makes This Country Great! #USA #Freedom #StarsNStripes #OldGlory #NissanSalesEvent!!!!

You never step in the same river twice, which is why it's so important to Instagram everything.

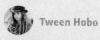 Tween Hobo

7/16

I think I might be the voice of my generation . . . or at least the voice of a gang of tramps that just got ditched at a Frisco depot.

Tween Hobo @TweenHobo   7/5
Life is like one crazy-long badass field trip.

....

Tween Hobo @TweenHobo   7/6
That thing where you stab a knife real fast between all your
fingers, and also you have a mani with an accent nail.

....

Tween Hobo @TweenHobo   7/7
If a Snapchat disappears in the woods, does it make a ringtone?

....

Tween Hobo @TweenHobo   7/8
She'll be comin' round the mountain when she FEELS like it OKAY.

....

Tween Hobo @TweenHobo   7/9
These hop fiends are ravin' but tain't nothin' compared to how
bad I want the Biebz.

....

Tween Hobo @TweenHobo   7/10
'Bo sleepin' next to me goes, "Shh, railroad dick's out patrollin'"–
and I totes snarfed juice through my nose like, Ew, you said dick.

....

Tween Hobo @TweenHobo   7/11
Down at the milk depot I'm all, "Do you have soy?"

Tween Hobo @TweenHobo   7/12
Shingles #IGotThis

Tween Hobo @TweenHobo   7/13
Dysentery #IGotThis

Tween Hobo @TweenHobo   7/14
Singin' "Polly Wolly Doodle" 24/7.

Tween Hobo @TweenHobo   7/15
Woke up this morning with a firefly hangover (that's what you get when you stay up real late watching fireflies).

Tween Hobo @TweenHobo   7/17
What is America's stance on the atomic wedgie?

Tween Hobo @TweenHobo   7/18
Siri, find me "Single Ponies" who are "Dappled" and like "Prancing." #graphsearch

---

Tween Hobo @TweenHobo   7/18
Now searching "Prairie Dogs" looking for "Activity Partners."

Tween Hobo @TweenHobo   7/19
If *Little Women* was written today, it would just be called *Tweens*.

Tween Hobo @TweenHobo   7/20
Snuck into public library to research Ninja Turtles; power went out; spent the night; saw a ghost; power came back on; Donatello's my fave.

Tween Hobo @TweenHobo   7/21
Will I ever get to have a bromance?

Tween Hobo @TweenHobo   7/22
Best part of a county fair is the rides; no, it's the livestock; teach the controversy.

Tween Hobo @TweenHobo   7/23
Morse code. Still a thing?

Tween Hobo @TweenHobo   7/24
Someone's in the kitchen with Demi Lovato.

Tween Hobo @TweenHobo   7/25
Every raffle I enter is an emotional roller coaster.

Tween Hobo @TweenHobo   7/26
Sneezed. #blessed

....

Tween Hobo @TweenHobo   7/27
When detectives take selfies, are they dick pics?

....

Tween Hobo @TweenHobo   7/28
Have you sent your mom an emoji today?

....

Tween Hobo @TweenHobo   7/29
Forever 21 used to be called 23 Skiddoo.

....

Tween Hobo @TweenHobo   7/30
Me, my selfie, and I.

....

Tween Hobo @TweenHobo   7/31
What is this "Space Jam"?

....

Tween Hobo @TweenHobo   8/1
Occupy Claire's.

Why, back in ought–six we had scads of penguin movies, simply scads.

⋛ ADVICE TO HOLLYWOOD ⋚

I'm pretty much an expert on pop culture and I'll be straight with you: best picture I seen this year was the symbol for "hot soup" carved in the dirt outside the station in Reno. So listen up, Hollywood, because I've got some suggestions.

Movies

- Next time we remake *Spider-Man*, let's focus more on Charlotte's web.
- Tell ya what movie I wanna see: *Biscuits 'N' Gravy 3D*.
- *Hobbit* schmobbit. Wake me up when they release a three-part epic of *Otherwise Known as Sheila the Great*.
- Once I've seen *Frankenweenie*, *ParaNorman*, and *Hotel Transylvania*, how will I have any regions of the human experience left to explore?
- Let's face it: *Home Alone* was the peak of American culture.
- You gotta go full Lincoln.

Television

- *Wither* (sequel to *Blossom*). #depressingsitcoms
- If I starred in a TV drama, it would be *My So-Called Hard-Knock Life*.

- Pitch: downtrodden rag dolls trying to make it on a personal and professional level in my new show, *I Just Want My Petticoats Back*.
- Just FYI, *Thomas the Tank Engine* presents a pretty sugarcoated view of railroad life.
- Bums kinda respect you more if you got HBO Go and you're willin' to share it.

Reality

- My new reality show is about dandelion seeds. Which one will be the last to blow away? And are they here for the right reasons?
- Based on what I've seen of reality, *The Bachelor* should be about a surly fisherman who mostly keeps to himself.
- They should make a Teen Wolf that's a documentary about an actual, very cool, very handsome teenage wolf. #justthefactsplease

Celebrities

- Been there, Halle :(RT@Gawker Halle Berry Will Miss the Oscars Because She Broke Her Foot Chasing a Goat
- Gwyneth Paltrow, dang, I ain't seen a lady that skinny since I hopped the westbound overland outta the Dust Bowl.
- Anne Hathaway's got a good old-fashioned case of ants in her pants.
- Hollywood is rough. One day you're hot, the next day Quvenzhané Wallis is three years younger than you and your tin can never rings.
- Chain gang's more work than Ben Affleck's marriage.

Celebrity Baby Names

- If Kanye named his baby North West, I'm gonna name my baby Thata Way.
- Why the heck did Beyoncé name her baby Blue Ivy? I tumbled in a patch of that once, itched like blazes.
- Snap, Crackle, Pop, Knox, and Vivienne.

☀ AUGUST 4 ☀

Los Angeles, California

Los Angeles. City of palm trees. City of sunshine. City of . . . death.

Folks, the situation is grave. I am gravely ill. In this city of glitz and tans I lie ashen and pale. My breathing is ragged, my cheeks aflame, my body speckled with a foreboding rash. Eleven and three-quarters years old and I may not live to see twelve. Illness has come and tapped me on the shoulder and wrapped its terrible arms around my small life. It's not consumption that I suffer from, nor mumps, nor tuberculosis. It is an ailment on a whole other level. Just when I was so close to finally finding my brother and restoring my family to health, *I've* come down with a dreadful case . . . of Bieber Fever.

My nurses (Stumptown Jim and the other guys) move trepidatiously in and out of my sickroom (which is a public restroom on Venice Beach). They fear I may slip away at any moment. My vision is half-gone by now, which means I have fifty percent more in common with Blind Hank than I used to. My hearing is not in great shape either, but that might be because I routinely listen to my iPod way too loud. Tin Cap Earl crouches beside me, beginning the laborious process of teaching me, with my new disabilities, how to "finger-spell." B-I-E-B-E-R, he spells on my palm. B-I-E-B-E-R.

My descent into this awful sickness began as soon as we hopped off the train in Bakersfield and began to hitch our way south. As we rambled down the sunstruck highway, a great bill-board loomed over our heads. The billboard was mostly purple, but for the beautiful peach outline of a certain youthful pop idol's perfect face. It said JUSTIN BIEBER. STAPLES CENTER. BELIEVE. I just about fainted dead away. By which I mean I jumped up and down and screamed and did six cartwheels. "It's happening," I panted. "It's really happening! Justin! Live! His hair! His hoodies! Oh my God—what if he brings me onstage for 'One Less Lonely Girl'?!?!! Oh my God. We *have* to go. We HAVE TO GO!!!!"

"I thought we were here to find your brother," said Stumptown Jim rather sternly.

"Yeah, yeah, we *are*. But also—JUSTIN!!!!!"

Jim sighed. "You know, I'm beginning to doubt the sincerity of your mission." And he gave me this *look*.

It was all I could do not to say, *Well, I'm beginning to doubt that you're not closely related to my fifth-grade teacher!*—but I restrained myself. And, on my phone, googled *Bieber tix*.

SOLD OUT, shouted Google. And I noticed they still haven't put up my SpongeBob peace-sign logo. Stupid Google. My throat started to hurt.

Here I lie, on the cold, grimy tiles of this once-grand public restroom. My head throbs. Somewhere in a Magnificent Palace of Staples, Justin Bieber tosses his hair and a tidal wave of girls' delight crashes upon the stage. Only one girl is missing. That is me. One More Lonely Girl.

Knowing I'm so close, yet so far, from Justin Bieber is surely what triggered this episode of desperate affliction. I've had symptoms of the Fever before—like when *Never Say Never 3D* was playing but Tessa and I had already seen it twice so her mom made us go see *We Bought a Zoo* instead. I got hives. It was bad.

But that was a minor flare-up. A common Bieber Cold, you might say. Not the full-blown virus. Not like this.

In my delirium, I begin to see strange visions. I see the doorway to an enchanted wardrobe, and I'm not even clear on what a wardrobe is. I see an Indian in a cupboard—and right next to him, a tiny Kim Kardashian, also in the cupboard. I see a little cake that says *Eat Me*. I eat it, obvs.

Suddenly I am transported to the Hollywood Walk of Fame. Pink stars with historic names like Paula Abdul adorn the concrete. The air is thick with glamour, and bus fumes. Captain Jack Sparrow from the *Pirates* movie franchise sashays up to me and taps me on the shoulder. His eyeliner is sticky in the heat. He offers me a twenty percent discount on prescription glasses or contacts at Pearle Vision. "I don't wear glasses," I tell him, "Oi, but now you do," he says in his fruity accent. "You got the Bieber Fever, me love. You're goin' blind."

Everything spins, and kaleidoscopes, and turns inside out like a reversible cardigan. In the haze, through strange rainbows, I catch a glimpse of Honig, my au pair, asking another tourist to take her picture as she pretends to eat Mickey Mouse's butt. I yell to her but she does not hear me. Justin Bieber's hair waves slowly in the breeze, like an amber wave of grain. I begin to cough up blood.

The sad thing is, I might die before I even get to first. Playing Truth or Dare with the hobos the other night, I said I had gotten to first already, but I was lying. I've never been kissed. I mean Frenched™. One time a boy at my Hebrew school kissed me on the cheek, but that doesn't count. And plus he moved to Florida.

More spinning. Then a thud. I am plunked down on some incredibly bright-green lawn, like the cleanest lawn you've ever seen, and in front of me rises a mansion befitting the contestants of a dating reality show. "What is this place?" I whisper. Then I see a sign, with an arrow pointing toward the mansion, and the sign says CELEBRITY REHAB CENTER.

I shake my head in wonder. *So this is rehab!!!* Could this be where my brother has been sent? The *celebrity* part is a little confusing because my brother's not famous, but then again, he is *pretty cool.* But if he *is* here, how can I find him? I decide to take a walk around and scope out the joint.

First thing I see is a giant swimming pool with a bunch of babes and hotties all hanging out around it. Everybody's skin and boobs are glinting in the sun. There's one girl just slowly pouring water over herself, shaking her hair from side to side under the cascade. It's super-inappropriate, and I feel like I should change the channel before my mom walks in. So I kind of dodge into some bushes and out the other side, and I find myself in a little secret-garden-type area where a group of young adults are sitting in a circle.

It takes me a second to I realize that I recognize every single face in the circle. There's Beyoncé. And Taylor Swift. And Kanye. And Lady Gaga. And Lil Wayne. And Miley Cyrus. And Drake. And Katy Perry. And Rihanna. And Justin Timberlake. And—sitting right next to Demi Lovato—with a pretty sour expression on his face—*is my brother.* EVAN!!!!!

His hair has grown out on the sides where he shaved it, but unevenly, in patches. He's skinnier too. He wears a couple beaded necklaces, and a T-shirt he stole from me that says DAD IS MY BFF. He's obviously wearing this ironically because all he does is fight with our dad, and also, it's way too small on him. Lil Wayne, who seems to be leading the group discussion, is holding some kind of conch shell and saying, "Life is like a box of chocolates. If you don't slow down for a second, you could miss it. Talkin' bout wee ooh wee ooh wee, okay, who's next?" My brother, nudged on by Demi Lovato, grudgingly raises his hand. Lil Wayne passes him the shell. Evan takes it, hefts it in his thin fingers, and goes, "Life is pointless." Okay—now I *know* that's my brother.

I come pirouetting out of the bushes and do a full-on body slam into the middle of the therapy session. Beyoncé is taken aback. Timberlake seems nonplussed. I don't have time for them. "Evan!" I cry in happiness. "I found you!" Evan looks at me as if through some kind of haze. "Dude . . . ," he mutters. "What are you doing here? Aren't you supposed to be at soccer?" All the celebrities roll their eyes at each other, light up electronic cigarettes, and the circle breaks up. I grab my brother's sharp elbow and try to tell him everything.

"I skipped town!" I tell him. "I been travelin'! A-wanderin' and a-ramblin'. I took up with vagrants, revolutionaries—like, hallelujah, I'm a bum! But my tramping's had a purpose—and the purpose was to *find you*. I've come all this way to find you, Brother—'cross the Great Lakes, 'cross the Mighty Mississip', cross the plains and prairies and Badlands and bayous! I've dodged railroad bulls, slept outside in thunderstorms, heck, I've survived on nothin' but crumbs and lip gloss! And sure as my bowl of mulligan stew, I knew I'd track you down. I knew we'd be together again, one fine day!"

My brother picks at a tiny hole in his T-shirt and rolls his eyes, just like one of the celebrities. "Okay, freak," he sighs. "Whatever."

"Evan," I plead. "What's wrong? Why did they send you away? And why aren't you happy to see me?"

"Stuff is going on that you wouldn't understand," he mumbles. "I'm seventeen now. You're just a kid. You don't get it."

"I'm not a kid," I protest. "I'm a *tween*."

"Gross. Don't use that word."

"But—Evan—listen!" I hear my voice start to get high and frantic. "I'm obviously old enough to get it. I've been traveling *by myself* for eight months! I slept in a cornfield! I ate squirrel—and I didn't even care when it touched some cabbage on the plate! I survived in the woods using nothing but my wits and freaking *Apple Maps*, dude! Do you know how crappy Apple Maps is?! I did all this to save you, my brother. I did it so"—and here I falter. "I did so—you would think I was cool."

Behind my brother I see Katy Perry sneer. Taylor Swift does that thing where you put an *L* up to your forehead with your thumb and first finger to mean "loser." Drake is like, "Yo, Evan, we bouncin'." My brother signals back to them, like, wait one second—and then he says to me, "I'm your big brother. I'm never gonna think you're cool. I'm like contractually obligated not to."

"But you used to," I said. "You and I used to be good buds. Don't you remember? I just want you to come home again—so things can go back to the way they were. Mom and Dad will snap out of their zombie trances, and you'll be nice to me again."

Evan was already walking away. "Sorry. It's just not that simple anymore. So stop following me around, okay? These are my friends and you're not allowed to hang out with us. You need to leave me alone. Go home. But remember, my room is off-limits. And don't touch my sneakers. Don't even look at them."

The force of my brother's total rejection knocked me flat on my back. I lay there, stunned, on the manicured grass of the Celebrity Rehab Center, which slowly congealed into the cold tile floor of the public-restroom-turned-infirmary. I heard Evan's footsteps, walking away. My head throbbed with pain and the bass line of

Bieber's "Boyfriend" remix by 2 Chainz. The cold tiled floor of the bathroom grew warm against my scarlet, hectic cheeks. What a sad way for a tween to go. Unloved. Unsung. Un-Frenched.

I felt a pair of hands on me. They were strong, smooth hands. Healing hands. Someone, I know not who, lifted my head up tenderly and nursed me with a few sweet, sweet drops of blue Gatorade. Onstage at the Staples Center, the Biebz sang my favorite line: "We could be starving, we could be homeless . . . as long as you love me . . ."

For a second I dreamed they were Bieber's hands. My eyelids softly fluttered open—or as softly as you can flutter your eyelids open when they're half-stuck together with pinkeye crud and eight-month-old sparkly mascara. As I blinked in the light, one sparkly tear ran down my cheek. "Hey, now," said the voice above me. "Don't cry. I know life's no picnic. But things'll turn out all right. They always do."

I sniffled. "Yeah, but, but I didn't get to go to the Bieber show. And my brother doesn't think I'm cool. And my throat hurts. And I've never been kissed."

The voice above me kind of chuckled, softly. The healing hands held on to me, with a firmness. And then, before I can even take a breath, a face leans down toward mine. The face has long hair attached to it. And lips as beautiful as a supermodel's. THE FACE IS THE FACE OF HOT JOHNNY FREAKING TWO-CAKES. AND GUESS WHAT.

I SWEAR.

HE KISSED ME.

OKAY, FOLKS?!?!?!?!?!?!?!!!!?!?!?

I HOPE YOU DAAAAAANNNCCCEEE!!?!?!?!?! RT IF YOU LOVE GOD?!?!?!??!!?!?

Instantaneously, as Hot Johnny's lips touched mine, my throat healed up, my skin began to glow, and my fever broke. It was like the whole world got BeDazzled. My heart and soul formed an ice-dancing pair and performed a flamenco as their folk-dance original dance. I won six Oscars and eight Golden Globes and four Tonys and twenty-nine Caldecotts. Even the tooth fairy was jealous of me???!?!?!!!!!! It was *BONKERS*!!!!!!??!?!??!?!

And just as soon as it happened, it was over. Hot Johnny Two-Cakes pulled away, quickly, as Stumptown Jim and Tin Cap Earl came barging in. "How ya feelin', kid?" said Jim, his voice brimful of loyalty and decency (the kind of decency that would *not* be cool with a random dude secretly giving me a smooch). "Oh!" I cried, startled. "I'm feeling much, much better!" Hot Johnny had already jetted out of the bathroom. I sat up and started pounding my chest, like a vibrant and hopefully adorable baby gorilla. Stumptown Jim and Tin Cap Earl looked superrelieved. "Sakes alive, kid, ya gave us a scare!"

I bounced up and fixed my ponytail. "You were talkin' in your sleep," said Jim. "Sayin' things. Strange things. Things about your brother."

The raging blue skies of my happiness at once filled with clouds. "Yeah. My brother. I dreamed we found him." The guys looked at me, curious.

"We still might," said Jim. "You said he went out West, right? Well, we're just about as far west as you can git."

"Yeah . . ." I shook my head. A tear fell from my eye. And Jim nodded and put his arm around me, as if he understood.

Tween Hobo @TweenHobo   8/8
Most Bratz dolls are staunch libertarians.

....

Tween Hobo @TweenHobo   8/9
According to Klout, I'm influential about Unicorns, Digital Lifestyle Technologies, and Dip (aka Chaw).

....

Tween Hobo @TweenHobo   8/10
"Gangnam Style" hit one billion views—and here I am with a hankering to watch it again.

....

Tween Hobo @TweenHobo   8/11
What's so suspicious about a kid in a dirty bowler hat not registered in the local school system trying to sign herself up for karate class?

....

Tween Hobo @TweenHobo   8/12
I have always depended on the kindness of park rangers.

....

Tween Hobo @TweenHobo   8/13
Nobody knows the bubbles I've blown.

....

Tween Hobo @TweenHobo   8/14
Stoically packing my lip full of Big League Chew.

Tween Hobo @TweenHobo   8/15
Ain't no spell-check on the raod.

....

Tween Hobo @TweenHobo   8/16
Wikipedia should have an entry about how long this spoon's
been stuck to my nose.

....

Tween Hobo @TweenHobo   8/17
This hunchbacked pool-hall rotation shark is not invited to my
bat mitzvah.

You can probably guess the *Hunger Games*
character I relate to most—it's Haymitch.

TWEEN HOBO TV SHOW PITCH

If they ever make a TV show out of my story, I think the show
should be streaming on Hulu and I think this should be Episode 3:

Episode 3: "Bat Mitzvah"

The train pulls into a Colorado station just outside Aspen,
where a billionaire Wall Street tycoon has rented out an entire
hotel for his daughter's bat mitzvah. The theme of this lavish
affair is "The Hunger Games," and when the guests see the ragged, dirt-streaked Tween Hobo loitering outside, they assume
she is a child actor dressed up for their entertainment as one of
Katniss's less well-known rivals (and, by the same token, assume
that Stumptown Jim is meant to be Haymitch). TH and Jim are

forced to compete in a terrifying dance-off and piñata battle for the amusement of the wealthy guests. When TH, infuriated, rebels against the powerful family by stealing some cake, Stumptown Jim accuses her of just being jealous. Tween Hobo has to confront the possibility that her own materialism and corruption have not been entirely eradicated by her decision to break free of the chains of capitalist society—and she also has to face the fact that, as a hobo, she will probably never get to have the vampire-themed bat mitzvah of her dreams.

TEAM HAYMITCH

 **Tween Hobo**

That empty oil drum is my office, and you, sir, just set fire to my fax machine.

#STUFFTWEENHOBONEVERSAYS

Still chuckling over that last Shouts & Murmurs piece, what a deft skewering.

I have a feeling that a real unicorn might ultimately be a disappointment.

No thanks, I've had enough Pixy Stix dust for one day.

Tween Hobo @TweenHobo 8/22

Boulder looks like the kinda town where a gal could redeem a coupon she won for a free roller-skating pizza party.

....

Tween Hobo @TweenHobo 8/23

Ice climbing. Picks or it didn't happen.

....

Tween Hobo @TweenHobo 8/24

Going to see a horse about a guy :/

....

Tween Hobo @TweenHobo 8/25

I'll tell you how we could get the housing market back on track: build more secret passageways.

....

Tween Hobo @TweenHobo 8/26

My Snapchats come and go so fast the government can barely get two screenshots of 'em. #privacy

Tween Hobo @TweenHobo   8/27

Life on the road has taught me hard lessons, but I still suck at fractions :(

....

Tween Hobo @TweenHobo   8/28

I like to give it a solid fifteen seconds between times that I say, "Are we there yet?"

....

Tween Hobo @TweenHobo   8/29

Cain't get a lick a' Wi-Fi in these jerk-water towns.

....

Tween Hobo @TweenHobo   8/30

Hot Johnny Two-Cakes' tweets are protected. Like I care.

....

Tween Hobo @TweenHobo   8/31

Time to catch "old dirty face" again. #Mondays

....

Tween Hobo @TweenHobo   9/1

Have you been living under a rock? Because I have.

MY GUIDANCE COUNSELOR

This was the look on my guidance counselor's face when I asked him if *he* ever had any problems with peer pressure:

He says nothing, but his eyes are clearly hinting I need more extracurriculars.

Teachers should never infringe upon my gum rights.

⇒ SEPTEMBER 2 ⇐

Denver, Colorado

As Stumptown Jim said, you can't go any farther west than California, so when we left there, we just turned back around. I was still reeling from my bad encounter with my brother. Fever dream or not, it was a punch in the gut. Not to mention that ever since kissing me, Hot Johnny Two-Cakes has been acting like if he even looks at me, he'll get arrested. Yep, things are tougher than ever. I'd be lying if I said my Tuesday underpants weren't ever so slightly in a bunch. And wait—it gets worse.

We pulled into Denver just as the aftermath of a school shooting was settling down. This school shooting was considered pretty minor, cuz only a couple kids got shot. Adults yelled at each other on the news, a few funerals were held with mini-coffins, they put the killer's face on the cover of *Rolling Stone*, and people more or less moved on.

Well, not me. I didn't move on. I felt sad and terrified.

But it seemed like even grown-ups didn't know what to do about it. The head of the NRA went on TV and made some fair points, such as, "The only thing that stops a bad guy with a gun is a good guy with a gun." Then he went ahead and blamed something called *Mortal Kombat* for the violence of society, which, I had to check with some old hobos to find out what that was (some ancient video game, IDK). He said all elementary-school teachers ought to be equipped with military-grade rifles and instructed to take out any odd-looking teenagers with extreme prejudice. (As a side note, I find it can be hard to tell the difference between a shy, troubled white boy who might murder my whole class, and one who I might just have a painful crush on.)

(As another side note: Anderson Cooper looks like the soul of a birch tree.)

It just seems to me that society needs to stop and take stock. I mean, I'm just spitballing here, but maybe—just *maybe—we should outlaw schools*???!!

Kids should have guns. Teachers should have guns. I should have a falcon. We should live on a desolate, war-torn planet. Eyes should be lasers.

In any case, the mood up here in the Rockies is pretty grim. So a few nights ago, as the last of the media vans were pulling out of town, and the grieving families were beginning to try to figure out what to do with a thousand memorial Beanie Babies, Stumptown Jim and I were frying up some grub. Over the crackle of the flames, unable to get the recent tragedy out of my head, I said in a small, fragile voice, "I'll never go back to school." I was about to add, *But I wouldn't shake a stick at a new Trapper Keeper,* when Jim cut me off.

"Now wait just a darn minute. I reckon it's September, ain't it? I reckon now's about when you should be startin' sixth grade."

I glanced up in alarm. It was like that point on the roller coaster when you get to the tippy-top, and everything slows down, and you know you're about to go hurtling into oblivion. Like that, except boring, instead of fun. "Oh, no. I knew this day would come," I said. "Don't you *dare* try and homeschool me, Stumptown Jim."

"Well, you're pretty far from home. So it wouldn't be home-schooling, now would it?"

"Homeschool, tutoring, whatever you want to call it—I'm not interested! I already got my *edumacation*! I know enough to survive on the road, and that's all I need to know. Plus, you don't even wanna eff with my learning disabilities. I'm telling you, I have the attention span of a fruit fly. And my Ritalin ran out way back in Truckee."

"Oh, so you think you're done learnin', do ya? Think you know everything?"

"Everything important, yeah."

"You know geology? You know physics?"

"The earth has one moon, and one Bieber. #Science."

Jim shook his head, not even acknowledging how cool it was that I had managed to verbally express a hashtag without actually saying the word *hashtag*.

"At least I'm not illiterate!" I shouted. "Most'a these bums can't even read a lick'a Lemony Snicket!"

"There's more to life than Lemony Snicket," said Jim.

"I'M WELL AWARE OF THAT!" I yelled. "There's also the great work of Sir J. K. Rowling!"

"I thought she was a woman."

"She *is* a woman! But she was knighted by the French government in 2009!"

"Lemme ask you something. If a train leaves Ashtabula going westward at a hundred miles an hour, and another train leaves Cheyenne heading east at ninety, how long will it take–"

"I DON'T CARE!!!!!"

"Hush now," Jim said. "You keep yellin' like that and we're gonna get caught out here. You don't wanna go to jail, now do ya?"

"I'd just as soon go to jail as go to math class!" I retorted. "Same freaking difference!"

"Well, now," said Jim in his plodding way. "I s'pose I can relate to that. Never was no good at math myself. But there is one subject I do hold in high regard. Can you guess which one that is?"

"Is it the subject of *broken junk*?!" I taunted him, then immediately regretted it. "Sorry. Too soon."

To his credit, he barely flinched. "Now there's no need to be unkind. The subject I'm referring to is History."

Almost against my will, I piped down for a second. I actually do like History. Or at least you could say I get a kick out of petticoats. Plus, I mean, slavery?!?! WHAT'S UP WITH THAT?!?!!?!

Jim took advantage of my brief silence to push his agenda even harder. "I propose that you and I take it upon ourselves to improve our minds and widen our intellectual horizons. In order to understand the present, and to be prepared for the future, we must gain a comprehension of the past. That's why History is important. And though they might be difficult, all those other subjects matter too. Besides, it ain't right for a kid like you to be runnin' wild without lookin' after your mental development. One day, you might need to take the SATs. And before that, most likely, the PSATs. So, kid. Whaddya say?"

"Okay, fine," I grumbled, giving in—and then a new tactic occurred to me. "But, Jim," I said innocently, "how are we going to protect ourselves?"

"Protect ourselves? What do you mean?"

"You know. In case there's a school shooting."

"Well, I don't think that's too likely. It's just gonna be you and me."

"Yeah." I scowled. "Exactly."

So for the last few days, me and Jim have been doing homeschooling. It's horrible. He gives me homework and actually expects me to *do* it. I'm now convinced beyond a shadow of a doubt that Jim and Mr. Brink are related. They say the words *pop quiz* with exactly the same intonation. Only difference is, Mr. Brink is more of a pushover. Jim actually gets mad when I don't come to class. And one time, when I sassed him, he made me sit in the corner of the boxcar for ten minutes *without my phone*. Until today, I thought that was as bad as it could get. But I was wrong. Seems like I've had nothin' but hard luck for a while now. And this morning, things hit a new low.

I showed up at our "classroom" (the burned-out campfire near Boxcar 9) over an hour late because I'd spent the better part of the morning creeping around the now-evacuated elementary school, scoping out the massive makeshift shrine that had accumulated there post-killing-spree. There were hundreds of candles and pictures of the dead kids. They were only a few years younger than me. It was gut-wrenching.

And something else was bugging me. There, on the sidewalk, just aching to be held, were about a planet's worth of perfectly untouched, fuzzily irresistible stuffed animals. It was a regular FAO Schwarz at that crime zone. To me, it just didn't seem right. Seemed senseless, in fact. What was the point of letting all those teddy bears sit there, gathering dust, out in the rain? Little angels in heaven can't play with teddy bears on earth, and besides, they're in *heaven*, which undoubtedly means they have toys out the yang. While I'm sitting here with jack squat. I mean, I still have my plush green M&M's guy, but I dropped him in a filthy puddle by the railroad tracks in Reno and now we're not speaking to each other. Look—this isn't even about *me*. Think of the Beanie Babies! Think of the Elmos, the Cuddlekins, the Care Bears. How do you think *they* feel, exposed to the elements, witness to so much grief, with nobody there to cuddle or snuggle them?! I'm saying, this is a borderline *Velveteen Rabbit* situation. They need my help. Which is why I bravely decided to rescue a couple of them.

So that was why I was late, because it took me a while to figure out which of the little fuzzy guys to snatch, and then I had to snatch them, and then I had to hightail it back to hobo camp to hide them with the rest of my stuff under a dirty army blanket. I was feeling heroic, but a little nervous, because I thought I saw a woman take a photo of me on her phone and then walk over to a cop. But we'll come back to that later, oh, trust me.

I get to class, and Stumptown Jim's all "Where have you been" and I'm all "Nowhere" and he's all "Yeah, sure" and I'm all "Don't you want to hear my report?" And he's all "Yeah, go ahead." So I begin to present my History report, which is on something called the Golden Spike.

"The Golden Spike—also known as the Last Spike—is the cer-emonial final spike driven by Leland Stanford to join the rails of the First Transcontinental Railroad across the United States connecting the Central Pacific and Union Pacific railroads on May 10, 1869, at Promontory Summit, Utah Territory. The term *last spike* has been used to refer to one driven at the usually ceremonial completion of any new railroad construction projects, particularly those in which construction is undertaken from two disp—disp—dis-pa—shoot. What the heck is this word?!"

"Stop right there," commanded Jim. "Just stop. Who do you think you're fooling!"

"Huh?" I blinked. "Who, me?"

"You didn't write this history report. You just copied it all down from Wikipedia!"

"Yeah, duh," I said, honestly confused. "How else would you expect me to do it?"

"I *expect* you to give it some original thought!" he thundered. "I expect you to care enough to put things in your own words!"

"But why?!" I countered. "What's the point? Everything's al-ready on the internet!"

"Listen, and listen hard. You need to get yourself through this life. You can't let other people do it for you. You need to do your own work and take your own medicine. The only thing you can truly call your own is yourself. And sometimes you can't even say that much. So be grateful every single day for the mind and the soul and the body you were given. Because that's all you got. And one day, even that will be taken away!"

"Okay," I said. "Take it down a notch."

"You need to learn *self-reliance*! That's all I'm tryin' to teach you! *That's* what's gonna keep you going out here, on the road!"

I looked at him skeptically. "Yeah, I guess. But you know, homey, sometimes I think *you* need to flip the script."

Jim was startled. "What are you tryin' to say?"

"I'm saying, maybe you should rely on other people a little *more*. Reach out to people. Don't just run away."

"I'm not running anywhere." There was that bracelet, tied tight to his wrist.

"Oh, no?" Summoning all my courage, I let the proverbial cat loose on the proverbial keyboard. "Jim. I know who your brother is. He's my fifth-grade teacher. Jeremy Brink. And he misses you."

Well, Jim practically fell backward off his log. His face was stunned. And then it was—angry. Angrier than I'd ever seen. He stood up, ramrod straight, and towered over me. His hands were shaking. "You got no business messin' in my affairs. You got no right to talk to me about my brother." Then he just turned and started walking away.

I was terrified. "Jim!" I cried. "Stop! Wait! Come back! I didn't mean it! Jim! Please!" But Jim didn't stop. And then I felt a vicious tap on my shoulder.

I whipped around to see none other than the woman who had taken the photograph of me down by the elementary school— and standing next to her, a lady cop. The cop said, "I think we found our girl."

The woman looked around at the campsite, the boxcars, the drunk, old hobos passed out under the trees. "This is unbelievable. She'll be better off in prison."

"Uh, what?" I asked.

"You're under arrest," said the cop. "You stole two stuffed animals from a public memorial. That's vandalism. You're coming with us." She clapped a pair of handcuffs onto my adorable little wrists.

"Jim!" I screamed, desperate. "Jim! They're takin' me down to the big house! Help me! Jim!"

Jim stopped. He turned back and looked at me, over his shoulder. He saw the lady cop dragging me away. All he said was "Save yourself." He walked off into the distance.

So, the upshot is, *I'm in jail now.* With no teddy bears. And no Jim. This is not a joke. I'm writing this from my jail cell. Thousands of miles from here, in Charlottesville, Tessa and the rest of the girls are getting started with sixth grade. To paint you a picture of how much jail sucks, I will just say this: I would rather be heading to math class with them.

Are you there, God? It's me. Tween Hobo. GET ME OUT OF HERE!!!!!!!!

Siri, why'd they throw me in the clink?

⇒ RAP GAME ⇐

In the first lousy jail cell they threw me into, down at City Hall, I met a cool dude named Florida Whitey, who taught me this saying *rap game.* You use it to indicate the vibe or flavor that you personally are bringing to the contemporary hip-hop arena. Here are some examples:

Rap Game Anne Shirley
Rap Game Nancy Drew
Rap Game Lumière, the Candlestick
Rap Game BFG by Roald Dahl

Rap Game Pippi Longstocking
Rap Game Disney Channel
Rap Game Chloë Moretz
Rap Game Soul Asylum
Rap Game Tavi Gevinson
Rap Game Shirley Temple
Rap Game Woody Guthrie
Rap Game Buzz Lightyear
Rap Game Willow Smith
Rap Game Judy Blume
Rap Game Pizza Emoji

What are some of yours? Tell us here in the comments. (JK, that's not a thing in books.)

Tween Hobo @TweenHobo   9/4
Nothing tastes as good as hobo feels.
....
Tween Hobo @TweenHobo   9/5
Soon as Hanukkah rolls around, I'll be flush with chocolate money.

Tween Hobo @TweenHobo   9/6

Who you tryin' to get crazy with, ese? Don't you know I'm lo-co(motive)?

Tween Hobo @TweenHobo   9/7

'Bout that soup-bone lyfe.

Tween Hobo @TweenHobo   9/8

I malinger at every opportunity.

Tween Hobo @TweenHobo   9/9

Mockingbird, do you have to be such a dick about it?

Tween Hobo @TweenHobo   9/10

The Cran·Grapes of Wrath

Tween Hobo @TweenHobo   9/11

I'll never forget what I was doing on 9/11: just chilling out in my mom's belly.

Tween Hobo @TweenHobo   9/12

I think I have a Friend with Benefits but he might be a Boyfriend with Drawbacks.

Tween Hobo @TweenHobo   9/13

In France they call me Le Tween Hobo.

Tween Hobo @TweenHobo   9/14

Hunger Games–theme bat mitzvah activity: electric slide till everybody dies.

⇒ SEPTEMBER 15 ⇐

Denver County Freaking Jail #smh

Welp, it's been a pretty sucky fortnight. A fortnight is two weeks and that's how long it's been since I got locked up in the penitentiary, aka the slammer. I'm writing this now from my cold, ugly cell, which I share with three other female hooligans under the age of sixteen. I was lucky enough to get incarcerated with some of the cooler, more popular Inmates at this juvenile detention facility, who quickly recognized me as one of their own and accepted me into their badass clique. So as far as my social life goes, things are actually kind of great. But as far as me *not being in jail* goes—things are about as amazing as bird poop. Before I tell you more about my cellmates, though, let me take you through my legal process.

Let's start with my Reese Witherspoon moment. That's when the cop arrested me and dragged me down to City Hall and I was like, "Do you KNOW who I AM?!?!" And they were like, "Uh, no, we don't, and please give us your name and age and Social Security number and contact information for your parents right away." And that was when I realized I better think up a good story, fast, because the last thing I wanted was for my zombie parents to get a phone call from this lady cop, which would only provoke their undead need to prove how "on top of stuff" they are and would probably result in their flying out here immediately to "get involved" with my judicial situation. No, I did not want that.

So I had to think up a fake name, on the fly, and for whatever reason the name that came out was "Clementine Obama." For that I received a lot of strange looks, and the cop pointed out that she had never heard of a white person with the last name Obama, and I retorted that it was an Irish name, and that she had left out the apostrophe, so that it was actually Clementine O'Bama. After that I demanded a lawyer and kept my mouth shut, so she just sighed and wrote *Clementine O'Bama* down on the form, and I tried so hard not to laugh that tears literally sprang up in my nose.

The next big to-do was my detention hearing. The judge presiding was a tired-looking, mom-haired woman who was obviously not buying any of my testimony but also did not want to be outsmarted by an eleven-(and-nine-tenths!)-year-old kid in her own courtroom. And I was slinging some serious hash. I probably won the Guinness World Record for most random lies told in one afternoon. My story made less sense than a Miley Cyrus video. I said my name was Clementine O'Bama, that I was from New Orleans, that I tween an orphan, that I was raised by wolves, that I possibly had magic powers, that my favorite color was orange (yeah right!?!), and that my favorite dinosaur was the stegosaurus (it's actually the pterodactyl). At a certain point the judge basically rolled her eyes, rapped her gavel, and said, "This is a waste of my time. This child is possibly guilty of theft and is certainly guilty of truancy as well as contempt. Hold her in County until she's prepared to provide us with a single verifiable fact. Next case."

So, yeah! I'm in *jail*, peeps. I've served fourteen days of my maximum fifteen-day sentence. Tomorrow they have to haul me into court again to see if I'm ready to talk. Which means I've got twenty-four hours to straighten out the backstory of Clementine O'Bama or else give in and fess up. Because I gotta get outta here. News flash: jail is the worst! The guards treat us like dogs, the other inmates are mainly scum and/or lunatics, and at snack time all we get are a couple off-brand Nilla wafers. I swear I'd cut my right pigtail off for a Snickers. Luckily my cellmates have a pretty phenomenal licorice stash.

As I mentioned, the girls I hang with are legit. Our ringleader is a beautiful fourteen-year-old with a chipped front tooth who goes by the name X-Box Mary. Word is she killed a man trying to get into Best Buy last year on Black Friday. Then there's Hot Pockets, a slightly grizzled seventh-grader who got busted for cracking open those plastic safes at Rite Aid where they keep the fancy shampoo. (In her words, she "cracked 'em open like ripe watermelons.") X-Box Mary and Hot Pockets bunk together, and over on my side I share a bed with Li'l Nikki, aka Dirty Nickels, aka La Femme Nikita. We don't exactly know what Li'l Nikki did, but she's sentenced to life (which is unusual for a ten-year-old), and I would not be surprised if eventually she works out some kind of deal with the government wherein she becomes a se-cret, ruthless assassin. Her eyes are pale, pale blue, and totally expressionless. She never smiles. She barely ever talks. She is the coolest bunkmate *ever*, and if we had a Jail Yearbook, I would write in it to her, *O.M.G., K.I.T., Luv 4-Eva, Never Change!!!!!*

Here's an example of how awesome my jail friends are. The other day, we were out playing softball in the prison yard, and I was pitching. *Accidentally*, I threw a wild corkscrew, underhand fastball that clocked the batter right in the face and broke her stupid nose. Because this batter just *happened* to be the same rat-faced girl who had hocked a loogie on my sponge cake the night before at dinner, it was *assumed* that I had thrown the ball at her nose in purposeful retaliation. The umpire (a prison guard) demanded that I apologize to Rat-Face, a request that I respectfully declined. Instead, I think I muttered something like "She knows what she did" and high-fived X-Box Mary. This was my mistake. The game was suspended and I was thrown in solitary.

Not more than half an hour passed in the hole before I heard some mysterious scratching and banging sounds in the darkness above my head. Ten minutes more and bits of the ceiling started drifting down into my eyes like gray snow. Hot Pockets had stolen a drill from the electrics closet, and these Bratz-level dolls had taken it upon themselves to figure out a way to sneak candy to me!!! Pretty soon the chink in the ceiling was big enough to slide a Pixy Stix through. They also lowered down some Red Vines, and a few candy cigarettes, which helped me relax. When I got out and thanked them, all they did was apologize for not getting the treats to me sooner. How sweet is that?!!

Yep, these girls are the best. I'm going to miss them when I get out of here tomorrow. Them being so nice to me almost takes the sting away from the fact that my best biffle in the known universe, Stumptown Jim, has deserted me. Almost. But not quite. Soon as I get back on the road, I'm gonna do whatever it takes to track Jim down and apologize for everything and—oh! It's lights out! I have to put away my diary and prepare for court tomorrow and listen to the sound of Li'l Nikki crunching on bird bones through another sleepless night. She catches birds that fly into our cell and eats them raw. I'm like, you do you, Li'l Nikki :)

Tween Hobo   9/16

That's so raven.

Tween Hobo @TweenHobo   9/17
Shivering in the cold wearing only a tattered shrug.

Tween Hobo @TweenHobo   9/18
Doing a Facebook Graph Search for "Wolf Packs" who "Live Nearby" and like "Human Orphans."

Tween Hobo @TweenHobo   9/19
Doing another Facebook Graph Search, this one for "Widows" interested in "Pie-Making" who like "Nut Allergy Awareness."

Tween Hobo @TweenHobo   9/20
Looking for a cool and responsible personal assistant to help organize my twigs.

Tween Hobo @TweenHobo   9/21
Atomic Fireballs are like candy to me.

Tween Hobo @TweenHobo   9/22
Edward Cullen is immortal. Me, I'm just immoral.

Tween Hobo @TweenHobo   9/23
Stars without makeup look just as pretty. #nightsky

Tween Hobo @TweenHobo   9/24
Siri, where can I pawn a miniature wood-and-metal ice-cream maker?

Tween Hobo @TweenHobo   9/25

They kicked me out of Girl Scouts cuz I was too good at starting fires.

Tween Hobo @TweenHobo   9/26

Oh, if only I could eat the pizza emoji :(

Tween Hobo @TweenHobo   9/27

This old dog won't stop yelping. Like I care if he got good service at some local bistro?

Tween Hobo @TweenHobo   9/28

At the racetrack, putting it all down on a My Little Pony.

Tween Hobo @TweenHobo   9/29

This white tree tried to get all up in my face and I was like "birch please."

Tween Hobo @TweenHobo   9/30

This poplar tried to leave me out of her clique.

Tween Hobo @TweenHobo   10/1

Slang term for a girl who you date because she's smart: your "thinkpiece."

Tween Hobo @TweenHobo   10/2

Spinning around in circles got me TURNT!!!!

Tween Hobo @TweenHobo   10/3

Tom Sawyer got me feelin' some type'a way.

I'm only twelve. But I'm a hard twelve.

⁊ OCTOBER 6 ⁊

Four Corners National Monument, AZ / CO / UT / NM (what what)

Four states at once. How you like me now?!!

It's my birthday. I'm officially twelve. And I'm at a truck stop in northern Arizona with not one single present and nobody here to sing "Happy Birthday" to me. Which is fine. I hate that song.

So, you're probably wondering how the crap I got out of jail. Well, it was easier than drawing a 3D cube (which I am good at). They hauled me back to the courthouse for my "community review," then proceeded, logically enough, to pay no attention to me. The judge was chatting with the lawyers in her Chamber of Secrets (copyright J. K. Rowling), and the two police officers on duty were busy grooming each other. Like a true drifter, I had my eye on the main chance—so when I saw the door yawn slightly ajar, I skedaddled. Just snuck right out of the courtroom, left the building, and tootled across the street to a Gap Kids, where I was able to shed my prison garb and reassemble my street look (jeggings and flannel), thanks to the beneficence of a broken-armed clerk named Jeannette, who, like me, had done hard time in the Denver Juvenile Justice System and was all, we are the 99 percent, let me get you that purple wash in a kid's-size ten. As soon as I was properly styled again and had thanked Jeannette for her kindness by tagging a bunch of hearts and peace signs on her cast, I dodged out through the back door and darted from alley to alley, till I found my way to the rail yards, instinctively. I never even heard an alarm go off at the courthouse. They were probably relieved to get the strange case of Clementine O'Bama wiped off their docket.

At the rail yards, I searched around for my homeys—Tin Cap Earl, Hot Johnny, heck, even Toothpick Frank woulda been a joyful sight. But I saw nobody. Seemed like I'd been ditched. Miles away, I could already hear the rumble of the next train approaching. In all my time traveling, I'd never yet had to catch out solo. Stumptown Jim had always been there, by my side, ready to help pull me up into an open boxcar or fight off a lousy railroad bull while I hid behind an oil drum. And now he'd left me, high and dry. Well, what was it he'd said to me? "The only thing you can truly call your own is yourself." I guess I was about to learn that lesson now, like for reals. Feeling superdepressed, I kicked the dirt. And then I noticed something.

Lines. Symbols. Hobo code. A message was written in the dirt.

I backed up to where I could make out the whole thing, and here's what it said, in translation: "Headed south. Catch out here. There are thieves about. Be prepared to defend yourself. Don't give up. Best Friends For Life." And it was signed with the initials S.J.

I wiped a tear from my eye. I was so happy to know that Stumptown Jim was out there, somewhere, and that he still considered me his BFFL, even though we obvs had issues. But on the other hand, where the heck *was* he?! "Headed south," he'd said, but that was pretty vague, and it wasn't entirely clear from his note whether he wanted me to come after him—whether he ever expected to see me again. It was tough having such a weather-beaten, taciturn adult man as my bosom friend. But Jim was Jim. And I loved him. And somehow, some way, I would track him down.

I heard the train, louder and faster, a-coming (that just means "coming"). Thinking fast, I deactivated the LED lights on my sneakers, so as not to attract unwanted attention. And I ran like blazes.

Aaaaaannnddd . . . now I'm here. In the desert. Or plateau, or whatever you want to call it. Basically, it's a truck stop just down the highway from the Four Corners National Monument. It's pretty desolate, just me and a few truckers and the Navajo elder who runs the convenience store. Oh—and there's also one of those inflatable dancing-tube guys. He's bright red, with flaming yellow streamers for hair, and a crazy smile. I've been watching him dance for an hour now. He has a strange kind of wisdom about him. I think maybe he's a shaman.

Which, if he is, I could use some spiritual guidance. I know I said originally that I was out on the road to find my brother, but things have changed. It's gotten complicated. There's Mr. Brink to think about. And Jim. Right now I feel like if I don't find Jim, my heart will basically implode. Anyway, the crazy tube guy knows all about my situation, because he was listening (and dancing) the entire time I was on the phone. Just now. When it buzzed and I saw my parents' landline number, I assumed they were just calling to say happy birthday and maybe, in their zombie way, to try and have a "check-in" with me about when I might be returning. But when I picked up, I got a big surprise. "Guess what!" said my mom, sounding human and alive. "Your brother is home!"

My heart thumped. Before I could collect my thoughts, my mom goes, "You're on speakerphone. Evan! Sweetheart! Come say happy birthday to your sister! And tell her how much you miss her, okay!" I heard a groan, and then footsteps. And then I heard my brother's voice.

"Happy bee-day, Sister Act. Where you been?"

"Evan!" I yelped. "Where have *I* been?! I've been out looking for *you*!"

"Well, I'm home now. You should come home too."

"Are you just saying that because Mom told you to? Or do you actually care?"

"Ha, ha." I heard him take me off speaker. His voice came through directly into my ear, familiar and ropey as the hammock in our backyard. "Hey. I actually miss you, okay? Who am I supposed to play Battleship with?"

"You hate that game."

"Fine. Then Mastermind. I don't hate Mastermind."

"Yeah." I looked up at Crazy Dancing Tube Guy. He smiled his crazy smile and jammed silently in the hot sun.

Evan coughed. "Listen. I'm sorry I messed up. I know it's been rough on you. But things are way better now. I promise. Even Mom and Dad think so."

"Are they being weird? Or normal?"

"Define *normal*. They're pretty upbeat. We've been binge-watching science documentaries together."

"Oh," I said, picturing it. "That sounds boring-slash-cozy."

"Exactly. So come home, will you? We need to stick together. I mean, since the bees are going extinct and the ice caps are melting."

I thought about it. Part of me wanted to launch myself like a Nerf Rocket all the way across the country straight into that supersmushy corner of the couch. But another part of me wasn't sure. If I went home now, I'd never find Stumptown Jim. Of course, I might never find him anyway, even if I roamed and rambled for the rest of my days. But what had his note said? "Don't give up." I didn't want to give up on him. And what about Mr. Brink? How could I return to Charlottesville without any proof that I'd found his long-lost brother? And speaking of Mr. Brink, something else was on my mind.

"If I come home, do I have to go back to school?" I asked my brother.

Evan repeated the question to my mom, who was still hovering in the background. I could hear her, so there was no need for him to repeat her instantaneous answer, but he did. "Mom says that's a yes."

Well, that decided it. I'm way too burdened right now to handle *that*. I have a lot on my plate. (Unfortunately, none of it is *food*, but I'm sure I can manage to scare up some grub—aka pinch some Combos from the convenience store.) "Cool," I said to my brother, lying through my teeth. "Sounds great. I'm coming home right away. Catch you guys on the flip side!"

"Wait!" said Evan. "Mom wants to know—where are you? Do you need to be picked up? Can you drop her a pin on Google Maps with your location?"

"Don't worry about me. I'll make my own way back. I'll get over the hump. It's tough, but I'm living fine. Got my eye on the main chance. And the sky's the limit."

"Wait—what?".

"GTG. Laters." And I hung up. Crazy Dancing Tube Guy beamed down on me, in total approval of my decision.

I stood there, in the blazing sun, secretly hoping that Tube Guy would speak to me. Tell me something. Where to go next. Where to find my friend. I clasped my hands in nondenominational prayer. "O Great Dancing Tube Guy!" I intoned (deciding it was best not to call him Crazy). "O wise one! I need your help! Guide me, o wise and inflatable one. Aid me on my quest!" I threw open my arms to the heat and emptiness of the sky, and I threw open my mind to the possibility of shamanic healing.

Then I heard something. A kind of singing. It was coming from the tube.

The singing, at first, was no more than a low hum. It might only have been the hum of the Tube Guy's motor-blower thingy—but then, suddenly, it raised and distilled itself into a voice.

The voice said, "Listen."

I threw my arms out even wider and called back, "I'm listening!"

The voice said, "Listen . . . to the wind . . ."

I listened hard, as if my whole body was an ear. (In which case I hope it would be pierced.) There was the low hum of the motor again. And then—a kind of—whimpering?

I got closer. Tube Guy whipped and twisted. The whimpering sharpened into a little howl. I realized that it was not coming from inside the tube, but from the patchy sagebrush at its base. It was a distinctly *adorable* little howl.

I whistled, not even daring to hope. And then my Worst Birthday turned into the Best Birthday Ever.

Out from the brush scampered a Dream Come True, in the form of a retriever-Chihuahua mix. A PUPPEH so drop-dead trusty and lovable that I can't even give her a name. I just have to call her the Greatest Little Dog in America. TGLDIA, for short. Stop the presses, folks. Picture an old-timey newspaper spinning straight into your face. Headline: GIRL MEETS DOG. DOG SAVES THE DAY!

Me and TGLDIA are standing on the side of the road now, trying to thumb a ride to somewhere with pancakes. I gave her a squirt of my Capri Sun, and she's wagging her tail in delight. I can still see Crazy Dancing Tube Guy, grinning in the distance. I'm a twelve-year-old ex-con and a dropout, but something tells me I'm doing everything right!

I'm gonna find Stumptown Jim, and in the meantime, I'm gonna survive out here like a total champ. Just me and my little dog. Hoboz 4 Life!

Tween Hobo Dos and Don'ts: DO wear UGGs with shorts; DON'T sell out to the Man.

THE GREATEST LITTLE DOG IN AMERICA

Look at my dog and tell me she's not TOLDIA.

I mean come on. She's criminally ADORABLE!!!!!

Tween Hobo @TweenHobo   10/8
The Colorado plateau looks like a desktop background.

....

Tween Hobo @TweenHobo   10/9
When does the selfie become the self? #philosophy

....

Tween Hobo @TweenHobo   10/10
Happened by a dig on the site of an old Southwestern village, found some pottery shards and a weird gray thing called a "Game Boy."

....

Tween Hobo @TweenHobo   10/11
How can this be a peace pipe? It doesn't even have any peace signs.

....

Tween Hobo @TweenHobo   10/12
Today I gave myself a Native American name: Little Feather Hair Extensions.

....

Tween Hobo @TweenHobo   10/13
I never pass up the opportunity to get my face painted.

....

Tween Hobo @TweenHobo   10/14
Traveling circuses can be more trouble than they're worth.

....

Tween Hobo @TweenHobo   10/15
Ran across a Gypsy woman. I think she got her scarf at Urban Outfitters.

....

Tween Hobo @TweenHobo   10/16
Reading my tweets aloud to these Gypsies.

⋛ KICKSTARTER ⋛

Name of Project: TWEEN HOBO'S LIFE
0 Backers
$1 Pledged of $1,000,000,000 goal, Infinity Days to Go (or Till I Die)

The Pitch

If Veronica Mars can do it, so can I. I'm a twelve-year-old self-producer, trying to get by in these tough times and stay independent. Help keep a grand American tradition alive—the tradition of me not starving to death, and also not having to do any math.

The Project

Surviving on the road. Evading the cops. Posting lip-gloss tutorials to YouTube. These are just a few of the many endeavors that make up the bold undertaking of my life. A life that you can support, with your donation, today.

So give something. Take a risk. It's worth it.
"If I'm scared, be scared. Allow it. Release it."
—*Beyoncé Knowles*

How Funds Will Be Spent

- 25%—Food
- 25%—Shelter
- 25%—Clothing
- 25%—Six Flags

As Seen In

- Denver County Juvenile Court Records, *Colorado v. Clementine O'Bama*
- Tessa Alexandra's Facebook Page, Top Friends List
- Milk Carton, "Missing Girl," Various US Cafeterias

Rewards

- Pledge $100 or more: get ten (10) fuzzy stickers, ten (10) oilies, and whichever of my sparkly hearts you want except the blue one
- Pledge $10 or more: get one (1) fuzzy sticker and one (1) Lisa Frank unicorn (previously stuck to my notebook, semiwrinkled)
- Pledge $1 or more: get one (1) sticker I peeled off a nonorganic lemon
- The greatest gift is the gift of giving to a celebrity's Kickstarter.

Tween Hobo @TweenHobo   10/17

So psyched to be in this Gypsy caravan—although technically I think I've been kidnapped.

Tween Hobo @TweenHobo   10/18

The Gypsies are favoriting all my tweets :) #kidnapped #NBD

Tween Hobo @TweenHobo   10/19

A nip of fall in the air reminds me that it's time to insert a full set of candy-corn teeth.

Tween Hobo @TweenHobo   10/20

Trying to calculate how many towns I can hit up for candy on Halloween with the North American freight schedules being what they are.

Tween Hobo @TweenHobo   10/21

People who just leave bowls of candy outside so u don't have to answer the door, I promise to honor yr system 100%. Where do u fools live?

Tween Hobo @TweenHobo   10/22

When I come to your house, you will have the option of giving me either candy or money for a good cause (which is candy).

Tween Hobo @TweenHobo   10/23

You bums can forget about me trading any of my Mounds for your Almond Joys. #NutAllergy #ImNotHereToMakeFriends

Tween Hobo @TweenHobo 10/24

Old hobos speak of a time when Halloween costumes weren't based on memes.

....

Tween Hobo @TweenHobo 10/25

You know what a sext is, but do you know what a *hext* is? It's a text from a witch.

....

Tween Hobo @TweenHobo 10/26

Montana Slim says he's going as the Yellow Guy from the "Gangnam Style" video.

....

Tween Hobo @TweenHobo 10/27

I might go as Slutty Anne of Green Gables.

....

Tween Hobo @TweenHobo 10/28

Diana is my bosom chum! #SluttyAnneOfGreenGables

....

Tween Hobo @TweenHobo 10/29

Slutty Anne of Green Gables hooks up with all the boys of Avonlea, not just Gilbert. I'm looking at you, Moody Spurgeon MacPherson.

....

Tween Hobo @TweenHobo 10/30

Some of my best friends are goblins.

⋗HALLOWE'EN⋖

(that just means Halloween)

I'm gonna come out and say it: Halloween is the best holiday ever invented. Sure, Christmas is kind of a rush, but then it's 6:35 a.m. and you've already opened all your presents and you don't have the right batteries and the stuff your brother got is better and besides, the whole Santa charade, it just gets exhausting. But Halloween? Halloween is *sophisticated*. Halloween happens at *night*. Halloween draws you into a tantalizing vortex of skeletons and *Scream* masks and animatronic tarantulas, and you know what's at the hot, pulsating center of that vortex? BITE-SIZE FRICKING SNICKERS BARS. THAT'S WHAT. It's like all the parents in the world took drugs and said, you know what, it's a school night, let's take our young daughter out on the town in a ratchet Disney Princess dress and full makeup and knock on everybody's door until this plastic pumpkin is filled to the brim with world-class Hershey's treats, *which she then gets to keep in her room, to be eaten at her discretion*. Whoever the freaks were that came up with Halloween deserve a Caldecott.

So I won't go into too much detail about what happened to me this Halloween, mostly because I'm having a hard time recalling specifics through my sugar haze. (I'm riding an empty grainer through Texas Hill Country, divvying up my tremendous candy pile with TGLDIA, who is *not* allowed to eat chocolate or, really, any of this stuff, so I get most of it, and she gets a piece of beef jerky, which is basically the Toblerone of the dog world, so she's psyched.) The key thing that happened was, I won a costume contest. Accidentally. And then all the kids in the town dressed up like me.

It went a little something like this. Having rolled into town on Halloween afternoon in the back of a Gypsy caravan (or, to be precise, a Dodge Grand Caravan driven by a polite Italian couple), I wandered into the parking lot of the Austin Jewish Community Center just as the kids were lining up in their costumes to be judged. I scoped out the competition and was impressed: there were your standard-issue witches, pirates, and Power Rangers, but also a spray-painted robot (homemade, #respect), a zombie Tinker Bell, and a two-headed girl who was really a pair of one-headed girls in an oversize University of Texas sweatshirt. (Which made me think—it would be tricky for Siamese twins to pull off a successful *Parent Trap* situation.) As the wobbly line of colorful characters arranged itself beneath the watchful eyes of grown-ups I assumed to be parents and/or rabbis, I emerged from the bushes in my tattered and filthy ensemble, mascara smeared under my eyes, hot-pink bindle perched over my shoulder.

A woman with craft-fair earrings and a fleece vest spotted me and held up her hand. "Hey, we've got one more," she called out, and motioned at me to come over. "Look at this—she's a *hobo*! Oh, that's terrific. Stand over here, Miss Hobo." The whole crowd turned to check me out, and I heard appreciative murmurs ripple through the parking lot. "Wow, she's so *dirty*," one kid said. For a moment I considered correcting their mistake and explaining that this was my everyday street style and that I was an actual hobo. But just as quickly I realized there was probably candy, or even cold cash, on the table here, and I might as well try my luck at nabbing a prize. So I lined up. The yarmulked Harry Potter next to me wrinkled his nose and shifted slightly to the left.

Obviously, I won. I mean I *swept*. Craft-Fair Earrings was the main judge, and she said my costume was so "terrific" she had to give me three prizes: Most Convincing, Zaniest, and Most Socially Relevant in the Current Economic Climate. When I untied my bindle to tuck away my candy booty (*booty* means "prizes," LOL), she oohed and aahed some more: "Look, she has a *railroad spike* in there! Oh, that's hysterical. That's a real period detail!" (When she said "period detail," I thought she was referring to my tampons, which I was still carrying, and I got embarrassed.) All the kids circled around me and poked at me and sniffed me and made awful faces and laughed and turned to their parents and/or rabbis and said, "She's awesome! I want to be a hobo!" I didn't think much of it at the time. I just grabbed my bindle and said shalom.

But to my surprise, later that night, when the trick-or-treating began, I saw that I had made *quite* an impression. Gone were the witches, robots, and Tinker Bells. In their place was a horde of little derelicts, each decked out in copycat rags, with an imitation bindle apiece. *Everyone was a hobo!!!!* It was *mayhem*!!! The neighborhood looked like District 12 from *The Hunger Games* on a bad day. And all these bums were angling for a handout. Door-to-door they went, knocking and begging without shame. I'd get to a house and the people inside would already be tired of me. "Not another hobo!" they'd moan. "What's this town coming to?!" And they'd toss an Almond Joy in my bucket and slam the door before I could say, "Nut allergy." It was infuriating. I wanted to kick the door back open and shout, "It's not fair! *I'm* the real Tween Hobo! These kids are all copying me!"—but that would only draw attention to the fact that my outfit was actually not even a costume in the first place. Instead, I just sighed and candyjacked a stray ladybug, who was too much of a baby to fight back.

Okay—but here's the twist. I turned a corner and ran into the lady with the craft-fair earrings from the JCC, who immediately recognized me. "Look, it's Little Miss Hobo!" she cried. "Well, aren't you a trendsetter!" She pushed her own daughter, who was toddling beside her, fully bindled out, forward to meet me. "Rivka, say hi," she commanded, and then, just making a general comment on everything, shouted, "Terrific!"

Rivka, who was a teensy little thing, approached me shyly. I inspected her. The costume was solid. Her hair was a mess, her face was dirty, and she wore a pair of overalls straight out of a Mary-Kate and Ashley adaptation of John Steinbeck. Most authentic looking of all was her bindle. It was made of a blue bandana—an old, distinctly *weather-beaten* blue bandana. "Wait a second," I said, freaking out. "That's Stumptown Jim's bandana!"

Rivka's mom, aka Craft-Fair Earrings, leaned in. "What's that? Whose bandana?"

"Stumptown Jim. He's my best friend, even though we got in a huge fight. I've been looking for him. That's his bandana. I'd know it anywhere! Where did you guys find it?"

"By the choo-choo trains," said Rivka, laying the teensiness on a bit thick IMHO.

"That's right," said her mom. "We went down to the railroad tracks, to get inspired. And we found this old bandana tied to a post. Isn't it just—"

"Terrific!" I finished for her, and tore off toward the rail yard. Now I knew for sure that Jim wanted me to find him. He was leaving messages for me! He had tied his bandana around that post so I would see it and know that he was out there, thinking of me. With TGLDIA by my side, her little tongue hanging out of her mouth like a small, wet rag, we ran through the dark, past clumps of hobo-fied trick-or-treaters, all the way down to the tracks, where we squatted in wait for a train to come.

We're on our way to find Jim now. The past is past. The future lies ahead. I do get to wondering, though, how the city of Austin is handling its sudden spike in child vagrancy. Sakes alive—I never said I was a role model!

If I, Tween Hobo, made a joke Twitter acct, it'd be a li'l raisin guy who dried up in the sun & was packing 2 pistols & doing bank heists, etc.

⧁ FAKE TWITTER ACCOUNTS ⧀

My own Twitter account is 100 hundred percent authentic and bona fide. I am totally opposed to putting anything online that is not accurate and real, because otherwise how is the government supposed to keep track of us all? Having said that, though, I do have a bunch of ideas for joke accounts, so here they are, and have at 'em.

Tween Hobo's Ideas for Hilarious Joke Twitter Accounts

1. Hot-Tempered Li'l Raisin Guy (@RaisinGuy)
2. Badass Bald Eagle in a Jean Jacket (@EagleDude)
3. Strict but Fun Governess (@MaryPoppins)
4. Single Eagle Who Just Wants to Get Married and Settle Down* (@0kEagle)
5. Sociopathic Yoga Teacher (@Namastank)
6. Proud Cat Lady (@CatPride)
7. Frontier Woman Kidnapped by Indians Who Is Kind of Getting into It (@HappyCaptive)
8. Eighties Businesswoman (@ShoulderPadz)
9. Slutty Ghost (@SlutGhost)

....
* A lot of my ideas are about eagles for some reason.

Tween Hobo @TweenHobo   11/3

This train is all Okies, Arkies, Texans, and sixth-graders (me).

....

Tween Hobo @TweenHobo   11/4

Who should I vote for if I want to keep my Nerf gun and also get a Nerf gun for my baby but not get married because boys are gross?

....

Tween Hobo @TweenHobo   11/5

If I made the laws, we'd pick our presidents the old-fashioned way: Funny Hat Contest.

....

Tween Hobo @TweenHobo   11/6

Dear Mrs. Roosevelt, how toned were your biceps?

....

Tween Hobo @TweenHobo   11/7

Writing a tragic American saga about homework: *The Grapes of Math*.

....

Tween Hobo @TweenHobo   11/8

The past ten years can be called a Lost Decade for the American Middle Class—and also for my missing Slinky.

Tween Hobo @TweenHobo   11/9
Gr8 Depressions are sooo depressing :(

Tween Hobo @TweenHobo   11/10
I go off a fiscal cliff every time I go near a Claire's boutique.

Tween Hobo @TweenHobo   11/11
Scrolling through Bieber's tweets, Johnny Cash "Hurt" on repeat.

Tween Hobo @TweenHobo   11/12
Gucci Gucci Louis Louis Fendi Fendi Burlap

Tween Hobo @TweenHobo   11/13
These rollin' Oklahoma hills are redonkulous.

When a man is starving, he won't really appreciate your scratch-n-sniff sticker collection.

NOVEMBER 15

Sallisaw, Oklahoma

To the red country and part of the gray country of Oklahoma, the last rains came gently, and they did not help what was already a bad hair day.

The hitchhiker (me) had traveled a long way, and now she walked down the dusty road, coughing a bit, hoping it wasn't strep™. Her trusty little dog marched beside her, flicking away the heat and flies with her tail. The dog was thirsty. So was the hitchhiker. And superhungry too.

A big, slow tortoise was crawling across the road, and it made the hitchhiker think of the tiny turtle in her fifth-grade classroom who still needed a name. Maybe, if she ever went home again, she would name it Zooey. Zooey Descha-shell.

The tortoise was taking its sweet time getting across the pavement, and now a vehicle was approaching—a white RV. The hitchhiker didn't think she could handle seeing that old tortoise get smushed. So she leapt out into the road and waved her arms in the air frantically. The RV came to a screeching halt.

All the doors popped open and out spilled a jumbled bunch of people that the hitchhiker supposed was a family, as opposed to, say, a rock band on tour. There was a dad, a mom, two older sons, a pregnant daughter, her skeezy boyfriend, two little children, and a very old lady. "What do you think you're doing?" shouted the dad. "You coulda been killt!" They seemed to pronounce certain words in the past tense like that. *Killt. Wisht.*

"You were gonna run over that turtle," said the hitchhiker defensively.

"Think I give ten cents about a reptile?" yelled the dad. "I got troubles enough! I got a whole mess'a troubles, believe you me!"

His wife tried to calm him down. "Now, Pa," she said, doing that weird thing where the wife calls her husband Pa. "She was only tryin' ta be a Good Samaritan. Ain't that right, little fella?" She seemed to be referring to the hitchhiker as "little fella," which was also weird, since the hitchhiker (me) was twelve years old and right on the verge of actually needing a bra. "Now, what on frying earth are you doing out here by your lonesome, little fella?"

The hitchhiker was about to answer, but she got distracted by the two little kids, who had come right up and started petting her dog. The dog, who was known officially as The Greatest Little Dog In America, seemed to take an immediate liking to the strange, towheaded little boy and girl and was licking their hands in a vivacious and friendly manner that made the hitchhiker feel possessive. She jerked at the little dog's rope to pull her closer, as the mom did a similar thing vis-à-vis the little kids. "Ruthie! Winfield! You two git over here, now! We got to keep the *fambly* together!" The two children, evidently scared of their mom, reluctantly backed off the dog and away from the hitchhiker.

The pregnant daughter was yawning a lot and kept trying to lean on her skeezy boyfriend, who was housing a bag of Late Night All-Nighter Cheeseburger Doritos and not really sharing. The very old lady was tottering around and mumbling ferociously about air-conditioning. One of the older sons was relieving himself on the side of the road, while the other, who had a more heroic air about him, came over and gave his mom a little shoulder massage. The dad whipped out his busted old cell phone to check the time. "Lookit," he said. "We're behind schedule. Everybody back in. Let's go."

"We cain't go, Pa," said the mom. "We cain't jus' up and leave a child on the road."

"Sure we can," said Pa. "She ain't our kin! 'Sides, we don't know who her folks are. Maybe they live round these parts. Maybe she's jus' walkin' home."

"Ain't nobody live round these parts no more, Pa, and you know it," scolded his wife. "Everybody's gone. Place cleared out. Us here is some of the last holdouts, and now we goin' too."

The little girl, Ruthie, started jumping up and down. "She can come with us! She and her little doggy!"

Before the hitchhiker could protest, Pa did it for her. "Heck no, she cain't," he sputtered. "We ain't got provisions! We cain't feed an extra mouth—two mouths, if you're countin' the dog! We ain't got enough to feed ourselves." And he looked as if he might start to cry. The more heroic older son stayed quiet but wiped his nose in solidarity with his father's pain.

"Well, now, think about it, Pa," said the mom. "Might be good to have a dog with us. Might be a kind of security. Gon' be stayin' in all sorts of who-knows-wheres, in camps and tents and all manner of backroads places. A dog at night could be a help to us. Might be a protector."

"Where are you going?" asked the hitchhiker, temporarily ignoring that these people were casually discussing adopting her dog, as if that was even an option.

"We're going to California!" announced the mom.

"Cal-i-for-ni-ay," enunciated Winfield.

"Oh!" said the hitchhiker. "Random! I just came from there."

Everybody stood up straight. The heroic son took a step forward. "You say you *been* there? Been to California?"

"Um, yeah. Like, a few months ago."

Gasps. Staring. The son spoke carefully, as if he was worried about his voice breaking. "You say you *been* there—been *all the way to California*—and then you turned around and *came back here*?"

"Um, well, kind of. I'm actually from Virginia? So I've never been here before. I'm just kind of traveling around. Trying to see the whole USA, you know?"

"Ain't nothin' to see round here," growled Pa. "Ain't nothin' but empty houses. Folks like us used to live in them houses, till the bank came along and kicked us out."

Pa's wife touched him sharply, cautioning him against exploding at a child. "Let Tom do the talkin'," she said. Apparently the heroic son's name was Tom.

Tom got down on one knee in front of the hitchhiker. She looked into his face. It reminded her a little of another face, the face of her missing friend, a hobo by the name of Stumptown Jim. It was just one of those faces that's seen a lot and found a way to handle it all without falling apart. The hitchhiker missed her friend Jim, and at the same time thought about asking this Tom guy if he had ever played MASH.

But now Tom was asking her a question. "Tell us, and tell us straight. Is there work out there in California? We seen a flyer said there's plenty work, picking grapes and oranges and peaches. We ain't scared'a workin'. Even the little fellas, they's ready to do they fair share. But tell us. There's work, ain't there? Out in that golden land?"

The hitchhiker didn't know what to say. All she had done in California was get Bieber Fever and lie on the floor of a public restroom chugging Gatorade and hallucinating about celebrities. She tried to think of something to say that would comfort this handsome, distressed young man in front of her, but before she could speak, his father burst in again.

"Course there's work," Pa spat. "We seen the flyer, ain't we? Said they need folks to come pick grapes. Well, we's a-comin'. Ain't no kinda work round here no more, but there's work in California. There's everything in California. California's the ticket."

The hitchhiker suddenly got a bad feeling about this family. Not about them personally, but about their situation. It was all very *Hunger Games*. They were in for some serious hard times. And then, for the first time since she'd left home nearly a year ago, the hitchhiker was seized with terrible guilt.

What was she doing out here, living like this, when she had a choice about it? When she had a warm house and a loving (in their own way) family and a fridge full of Ocean Spray and even her own little piggy bank containing US $45.68 and a bunch of French francs from when her dad went to Aix-en-Provence to speak at a conference there? What kind of scam was she trying to pull here? She felt like a vulture, feeding on other people's problems. Worse than a vulture—she felt like her au pair. A tourist.

Ruthie, the little girl, had crept back over and started petting the dog again. The hitchhiker didn't jerk the rope this time. Tom was still kneeling before her, waiting for an answer. "Tell us," he said again. "What's it like out there? In California?"

She took a deep breath and considered lying, but honesty overcame her. "Um, it's okay. I mean, there's Disneyland and stuff. And it's nice out. But it's not that different there from anywhere else. They have Starbucks. They have Trader Joe's. It's kind of–whatever. Basically."

The family took this in. The pregnant daughter yawned again and said to her skeezy boyfriend, "You can get a job at TJ's." He nodded vaguely and tapped the spicy dust at the bottom of his Doritos bag into his mouth. The old lady had already climbed back up into the RV. The tortoise, by this point, was already across the road and slowly vanishing into the high weeds.

Pa stomped his foot and gruffly commanded, "Back in the van now, Ma. We behind schedule. We got to git moving. Got to get to Texas before dark."

"What about the child?" asked Ma, but the hitchhiker now spoke up on her own behalf.

"No, no, it's cool–I'm fine. I actually need to be heading East. My family's back that way, and they probs miss me." As if on cue, the hitchhiker's bindle buzzed. "LOL, I bet that's my mom texting me right now. She's kind of psychic like that."

The Greatest Little Dog In America was now fully curled up in Ruthie's arms. "Come on, Ruthie," said Tom. "Leave the dog. We got to get back on the road." Ruthie's eyes filled with tears.

The hitchhiker made a snap decision. "You can take her. She likes you. And she can protect you–like you said. At night." Having made this offer, the hitchhiker swallowed, trying not to cry.

Ruthie and Winfield clapped in delight.

Ma nodded approvingly. "That's real kind'a you. What do you

think, Pa? Think we kin take her? I mean—long as the child's sure 'bout giving her away."

"I'm sure," said the hitchhiker. The little dog wagged her tail, as if agreeing to the plan.

"Oh, Pa, kin we take her? Please?" clamored Ruthie and Winfield.

"Well, now, I s'pose," growled Pa. "S'pose we could use a dog to guard our tent. Don't know what we'll feed her, but, heck. S'pose Providence will look after us somehow."

Ruthie and Winfield jumped for joy. The hitchhiker, with a full heart, hugged her little dog good-bye, taking a moment to enjoy one last slobbering doggy kiss. "Take good care of her," she said to the kids. "She likes Skittles, but she's really not allowed to eat them."

Tom took hold of the dog's fraying rope leash. "We'll look after her. Don't you worry. She's one of us now. One of the Joads." And the setting sun burnished his strong profile, like a president on a nickel.

Ma reached into her pocket, which was empty. "Wisht we could give you somethin' in return," she lamented. "But we ain't got nothin' to give."

"Don't worry about it," said the hitchhiker. "I'm psyched to help you guys out."

"And ain't that the secret," said Ma. "Ain't that the whole mysterious secret, right there."

Then everybody was climbing back into the RV. The sun was setting on the Oklahoma countryside. Another day in America was drawing to a close, and the Joads were getting back on the road.

As the family pulled away, the hitchhiker heard her little dog howling farewell. She noticed two bumper stickers on the back

of the RV. One said MY KID IS AN HONOR STUDENT AND MY PRESI-
DENT IS A MORON. The other said THERE'S ALWAYS MONEY IN THE
BANANA STAND. The hitchhiker laughed at this one and ambled
along in a northeastern direction.

Tween Hobo @TweenHobo   11/16

Pretty sure I'm writing the Great American Novel. Then again I mostly read Bazooka wrappers

....

Tween Hobo @TweenHobo   11/17

One day I'll git me a mighty fine padded bra.

....

Tween Hobo @TweenHobo   11/18

The best paninis in life are free.

....

Tween Hobo @TweenHobo   11/19

When a man's shamed of his beggin' ways, he's all "No hobo."

....

Tween Hobo @TweenHobo   11/20

Whistlin' "Dixie," scribblin' yin-yangs.

....

Tween Hobo @TweenHobo   11/21

Oh, I wish I was in the land of cotton, or even cotton-Lycra-blend!

....

Tween Hobo @TweenHobo   11/22

What kind of peddler doesn't have any slap bracelets?!?!

....

Tween Hobo @TweenHobo   11/23

I find that parkour never goes as well as I'd expected.

....

Tween Hobo @TweenHobo   11/24

Remember, it's not Thanksgiving until somebody gets trampled at a Best Buy.

....

Tween Hobo @TweenHobo 11/25

I'm thankful for the guys who blow up the Macy's Hello Kitty balloon.

....

Tween Hobo @TweenHobo 11/26

Before the internet I s'pose folks looked for simpler ways to spend their Cyber Monday.

In the old days, kids would go from house to house, just crushing all the Hamburger Helper they could find.

HOW TO MAKE MULLIGAN STEW

Mulligan stew is a classic hobo dish, and it takes a team effort. That's what makes it fun! (And perfect for sleepover parties.) Here are the simple steps you and your roughneck clique of BFFLs can follow to make a mulligan.

- Gather all the available hobos together for a hobo huddle. You might want to kick things off by putting all your hands in the middle of the circle and cheering, "Goooo . . . hobos!" Or "Souuuuuupp!" Or whatever.
- Assign tasks. One hobo stays at the campsite (or mom's kitchen) and builds the fire (or asks permission to use the stove). Others are responsible for rustling up the ingredients, as follows . . .
- Meat. Potatoes. Onions. Bread. If a chicken can be stolen, awesome. If you want to throw in a couple gluten-free vegan meatballs, go for it. The whole point of mulligan stew is that it's open to interpretation. No two mulligans are alike. Like fingerprints. Or Olsen Twins, if you look carefully. Which brings us to . . .
- Google. The essential ingredient in any modern recipe. Because, if you want to find an actual recipe for mulligan

stew, use Google. I'm not writing a cookbook here. So, in short . . .

- Do whatever the internet tells you, which, it probably involves salt. And then when it's all cooked up, dig in! There should be enough to go around, if you made enough, which I hope you did, even for the less popular hobos in your group. Remember that Jennifer Lawrence was not popular in middle school. So you never know. And also remember . . .
- Beans. They just make everything better.

And THAT'S how you make a mulligan stew!
(Ish.)

Tween Hobo @TweenHobo 11/28

I know #FF stands for Follow Friday, but what is the abbrev for when you switch bodies with your mom (*Freaky Friday*)?

....

Tween Hobo @TweenHobo 11/29

A solid internet relationship's liable to go bust if you run across the fella IRL.

....

Tween Hobo @TweenHobo 11/30

Read the Wikipedia page on *Tom Sawyer*, thinking of setting up my own fake funeral.

....

Tween Hobo @TweenHobo 12/1

Trying not to be a bridezilla about my fake funeral.

....

Tween Hobo @TweenHobo 12/2

Will it be obvious I'm not actually dead if I live-tweet my own fake funeral?

....

Tween Hobo @TweenHobo 12/3

When the kid you tricked into painting the fence shows up at yr fake funeral. #awkward

Tween Hobo @TweenHobo   12/4

You really have to seize opportunities in life to make the *Home Alone* face.

Tween Hobo @TweenHobo   12/5

How come boys always want to know if you have a dowry?

Tween Hobo @TweenHobo   12/6

Waiting for the Victorian Silhouette filter on Instagram.

Tween Hobo @TweenHobo   12/7

What the shucks?!!

Tween Hobo @TweenHobo   12/8

My superpower is making the same outfit look good two hundred days in a row.

Tween Hobo @TweenHobo   12/9

I've had it with all these robber barons.

Tween Hobo @TweenHobo   12/10

LOL at naked guys in barrels.

Tween Hobo @TweenHobo   12/11

All I want for Christmas is my two front teeth, plus a blinged-out grill to put over them. #ice #krunk #hustla

Pro Tip: Minesweeper = more fun than actual mining.

⋛ DECEMBER 12 ⋚

Boone County, West Virginia

By now everybody's seen the footage—the story aired around the clock while we were trapped, and since our being safely extracted, they haven't moved the cameras off my face. Much has been made of the fact that the Mud River Coal Company dim-wittedly hired a preteen girl disguised, by means of a penciled-on mustache and a *very* fake-sounding accent, as a small Latino man. Huge bribes have been offered by the media to said girl (whose mustache was mostly wiped off by the time she and her comrades emerged from the collapsed mine after their days-long ordeal) in exchange for revealing the sordid details of what really went down, *way* down, down there in the mine. All of these bribes have been refused, in honor of the "pact of silence" that the thirteen trapped miners (including me, Tween Hobo) swore ourselves to while we were underground. There are some things we will not speak about. Not even in our diaries.

Here's what I will tell you: Half a mile below the earth's crust, where it's always dark as night and what little air there is to breathe tastes like dinosaur farts, you must rely on your fellow man to survive. Civilization is crucial underground. Up on the surface, we can act like animals and get away with it. But down below, we have to behave ourselves. As one headline put it, "Trapped Miners Formed Micro-Society to Keep Themselves Sane." We sure did. It was like a well-run after-school program down there. We had jobs. Activities. A strict schedule that went something like this: Breakfast. Prayers. Clearing debris. Snack. Seven to eight hours free time. Another snack.

Here's what else I'll tell you: Getting trapped in a mine is a kick-ass way to get famous. Go ahead, start your own YouTube channel, build a social media presence, and so forth, but for instant celebrity, nothing beats a near-fatal mining accident. When I finally got "topside" yesterday, it was not only with my life. It was with a book deal and film options. Booyah.

But of course, the best part of yesterday had nothing to do with licensing opportunities or seeing that my name (along with the name of the mine, Boone Coal Mine 1A) was trending on Twitter—or even with the dazzling sensation of the sun hitting my face for the first time in almost a week. It was an even more dazzling sensation. It was when I opened my eyes and blinked and saw who was camped out there, at the mine's busted entrance, waving a little American flag and waiting for me. Who else but my homey of homeys: Stumptown Jim!!!!!!!!!!

I searched for the words to express my joy, but Jim took the lead and spoke first. "Way to go, kid," he said in an unwavering voice. "You made it. Had me worried there." And he opened up his arms and gave me an emotional, patriotic hug.

"Jim!" I cried. "How did you find me?"

"Saw you on TV. You been all over the news. The *New York Times* website has a little interactive timeline of your life. On the home page."

I nodded, pretending to be dazed by all the attention, while secretly loving it. "Oh, Jim!" I pressed his hand to my cheek affectionately, if also aware that it would make a nice shot for the reporters. "Oh, I've missed you so!"

"You been through a lot since I seen you last," said Jim, studying me as the rescuers unclipped my safety harness. "Seems like you've changed."

"Well, I'm twelve, for one thing. Twelve and two-twelfths." I flagged the rescuer, who was walking away. "Hi, yeah—can I get some water? . . . No—not Dasani, God no. SmartWater, if you have it. Something with electrolytes?" I turned back to Jim. "Sorry—you were saying?"

"Yeah, you sure do seem grown-up."

"Well, thanks," I said, motioning to Diane Sawyer and her team that I would be there in a few.

"I gotta admit," Jim continued, "when I ditched you back there in Colorado, I didn't expect you to keep on train-hopping by yourself. Thought you'd be on Travelocity in no time, booking yourself a discount flight home. But you proved me wrong. You got mettle, kid. Moxie. Grit."

"I wouldn't go home without finding *you*. And besides, you knew I was still riding the rails. You wrote me that note in the dirt back in Denver. And your bandana, in Austin. You left it there for me."

"So you found it. Well, I'll be." The light in Jim's eyes crackled like the warmest campfire.

Just then we were interrupted by my new manager, Todd, who I'd signed with via vacuum-sealed tube while still in the tunnel. Todd gets 15 percent of net received and will represent me across all platforms. He has a goatee. He approached me now with one BlackBerry glued between his shoulder and ear and another one outstretched for me to take. "It's your dad. I told him he could have five minutes. After that it's Diane, and then I'm gonna need you to look over some endorsement packages." I took the phone. Jim looked suspicious. Meanwhile, my father was eagerly shouting at me.

I'm sure it had nothing to do with the book deal or the Capri Sun sponsorship, but suddenly my dad was *very* insistent that it was time for me to come home. He also wanted to know if Clooney was available to play him in the movie. I didn't have the heart to tell him that Clooney had already signed on to play our brave foreman, Ernesto. Dad put me on speaker and the whole family pleaded with me to come home for Christmas slash Hanukkah. Even Evan was getting hysterical.

I interrupted them. "You guys. Listen. I'm *trying* to come home. That's how I got into this mess in the first place. I realized in Oklahoma that I needed to come home, but I didn't have any money, so I started looking for work, and the first job I found was this mining gig here in Boone County. Which, obviously that didn't work out very well. But now I got this book deal and everything, so I'm flush, and I'm heading home right away! I'll be there to light the menorah, I promise. . . . No—I don't need you to pick me up, Mom. I'll get home my own way. But don't worry—I'll make it. Love you guys." I hung up and smiled at Jim, who was gazing upon me with pride.

"Guess you learned that lesson I was trying to teach you," said Jim.

"Which one? I still suck at fractions."

"Self-reliance."

I blushed, honored at his praise, and lifted my chin slightly, trying to achieve the look of a noble mouse sailing a tiny birchbark boat.

"And there's something else I wanted to tell you." Jim coughed. "I been thinkin' on *your* lesson too. The one you were tryin' to teach me. And I think I get it now. And I'm ready."

"Ready for what?" I asked.

"Ready to see my brother."

I swear I couldn't have been more excited if you'd told me Justin Bieber had successfully been cloned. Suddenly, all the pieces of my strange journey seemed to add up and amount to something. I was going to reunite two long-lost brothers. I was going to Heal What Was Broken in This Land. I was going to be Mr. Brink's favorite . . . for life. This was even better than when Hot Johnny kissed me. This was like getting kissed by US president number 12, Zachary "Z-Tay" Taylor, himself.

But before I could whoop and holler to an appropriate degree, my new manager, Todd, had gotten in the way. He squeezed in between us, wrapped his arm around me, and panted heavily into my ear. "There's two million on the table. Two mil, baby. And all you have to do is talk."

"Talk about what?"

"Oh, you know," exhaled Todd. "Stuff. Your time on the road. Your favorite colors. *The pact of silence.*"

I pulled away sharply. "What do you mean, the pact?"

"I mean, oh, just, come on. We're talking two million here. All yours if you tell them what went on down there."

"But—we swore a holy oath. I can't betray my fellow miners."

"Come on—oath shmoath. One of these guys is gonna crack. And if it's you, then you walk away with the cash. Hey—it doesn't even have to be true. You can make something up! It just has to be *entertaining.*" Every part of Todd seemed to be wiggling. His goatee was all over the place.

Jim could tell something was wrong. He broke in, "Hey, kid. Who is this guy?"

Todd sized Jim up through his tinted glasses. "Excuse me, who are you?"

Jim said, "I'm her friend."

Todd said, "Well, I'm her *manager*."

I decided to go with my gut. "No, Todd. You're fired."

Todd goes, *"What?!"*

I turned to Jim. "Jim, do you think you could handle being my manager?"

Jim goes, "Reckon I could do that, sure."

I said, "Great. Diane Sawyer gets ten minutes. Then we're outta here. We need to get home for the holidays."

Todd, who was dripping sweat, goes, "This is so unprofessional!"

Jim goes, "Do you want me to kill this guy? With my bare hands?"

I go, "No, that's not necessary," and led Jim over to the ABC News tent, where Ernesto and the rest of the miners were getting foundation applied. The interview was over in a flash, and then Jim and I ran for the hills. Dang, it feels great to be back on the road with my BFFL!!!! And we're almost home!!!! *L'chaim!!!!*

Tween Hobo @TweenHobo   12/13

Have my people call Honey Boo Boo's people, set up a meeting in a ditch.

....

Tween Hobo @TweenHobo   12/14

If *Hannah Montana* was based on me, it'd be called *Billings Montana* and there'd be a heck of a lot more mining involved.

Tween Hobo @TweenHobo   12/15

None of the other stowaways on this steamboat have gotten to first ;)

....

Tween Hobo @TweenHobo   12/16

For a stowaway on a steamboat it's safer to be a boy. So my hair is tucked up in my cap and I'm whining about *Minecraft*.

....

Tween Hobo @TweenHobo   12/17

Stowed away on this steamboat, waves lulling me to sleep, just like the sweet wayback of my mom's Kia Sorento.

....

Tween Hobo @TweenHobo   12/18

Heard one of the other stowaways say something about "child slavery"; now pulling into harbor, squeezing my stress ball.

....

Tween Hobo @TweenHobo   12/19

Pulling into harbor, about to be sold into child slavery, but I won't go! Mutiny! Mutiny and then hopefully some snorkeling, I say.

....

Tween Hobo @TweenHobo   12/20

Chugging smuggled Four Loko in preparation for steamboat mutiny.

....

Tween Hobo @TweenHobo   12/21

Might as well call that ship the HMS *Suck It*. #EnufAlready

....

Tween Hobo @TweenHobo   12/22

Stumptown Jim's an atheist, but me, I'm a #Belieber. IS IT CHRISTMAS YET??!?!?!!

I'm gonna light up this town with my
Christmas spirit! And with my light-up Heelys.

⊰ DECEMBER 23 ⊱

Charlottesville, Virginia, aka Home Sweet Home
(well, actually, School)

Jim and I emerged from the woods behind the school today at around 11:30 a.m., just as the James Monroe Upper Elementary Winter Community Sparkle Event was getting under way. (You could call it a Christmas pageant, if you wanted to probably get sued.) We snuck into the gym through the back doors just in time to catch the end of the fifth grade's performance, a stirring dramatization of the labor conditions of elves. And then it was time for the sixth grade to go onstage—led by none other than my teacher, Mr. Jeremy Brink. Hearts!!!!!

As Mr. Brink ushered his class onstage (Tessa in the lead, wearing a knitted Jonas Brothers sweater and holding a red-and-green Kwanzaa kinara), I saw a wave of something like panic cross over Stumptown Jim's face. "That's him, isn't it?" I said.

"Yeah," said Jim. "That's my brother. Shoot. I don't know if I can do this." He shrank backward, as if he wanted to disappear into the gymnasium wall.

"Sure you can!" I whispered, afraid he was going to bolt back out to the woods.

"*Sshh,*" said somebody's mom, who was sitting in the back row of folding chairs. She turned around to glare at us, and so did a few other people who occupied various points on the parent-teacher-student triangle. I tried to make myself inconspicuous. And then Jim knocked over a giant rack full of basketballs.

The rack crashed to the ground and the balls went bouncing everywhere, and the entire audience twisted around to see what had happened. The Winter Community Sparkle Event was momentarily on hold. Tessa, onstage, caught sight of me all the way in the back, dropped the kinara, and shrieked. Mr. Brink stared.

We must have made quite a picture, me and Jim, with our bindles and our raggedy clothes—and quite a stench too. We would probably have been thrown out of the gym if not for the fact that I was famous now, and had been on TV so much over the past few weeks that everybody simultaneously recognized me. "Oh my God, it's that poor little girl from the mine!" I heard multiple people say. "She's a local!" said someone else. "She ran away from home!" "She ran away from *this school*!" "Who's that guy with her?" "He looks like some kind of *freegan*!" "Who *is* he?"

Mr. Brink's voice shot through the hubbub: "He's my brother!" And he marched down off the stage and strode toward us. Jim looked supernervous. I saw his Adam's apple bob a little.

The whole audience would gladly have turned their seats around and watched the scene that was about to take place between me, Mr. Brink, and Jim instead of the rest of the Sparkle Event, but Tessa, refusing to be outshone by my glorious return, struck up the band onstage. My former classmates rang their wrist-strapped bells and began a loud rendition of "The Twelve Days of Christmas." The audience tuned in, but Mr. Brink paid no attention. He grabbed both Jim and me by the arms and led us out of the gym. I managed to turn around and stick my tongue out at Tessa real quick before we left.

———————————

In the sixth-grade homeroom, it was as quiet as paper snowflakes. Mr. Brink sat at his big teacher's desk, and Jim and I sat at two little desks in the front row, facing him. I felt like I was watching a special episode of a reality show about two brothers who haven't spoken in fifteen years—or, actually, more like I was watching the uncut footage, before they edit it and make it entertaining. The Brink brothers' real-life reunion could have used a lot more smash cuts and "Say whaaa??"-type sound effects. In its raw form, it was kind of excruciating. There was a lot of silence, or they would start to say something at the same time, and Jim would go, "You first," and Mr. Brink would go, "Sorry"—at which point they'd fall mute again. Finally Mr. Brink got out a whole sentence: "I barely recognize you."

Jim squirmed in his little desk. "I know. I look like hell."

"No matter what you look like, it's been fifteen years." They fell into another long, awkward pause. Then Mr. Brink said, "But you do look pretty awful."

Jim squinted and ran a finger through his beard.

Mr. Brink goes, "You look like an old porcupine."

Jim stiffened. "Okay."

I go, "Dang, Mr. B. You *went there*."

Mr. Brink turned on me. "You don't look so good yourself, kid. And you smell like garbage."

"Don't pick on the kid," said Jim. "She's been through the wringer, I'll tell you."

"I don't think it qualifies as 'picking on her' to point out that she's missed an entire year of school, and that her general appearance and hygiene level do not comply with this school's expectations for our Winter Community Sparkle Event." Mr. Brink was sounding like kind of a nerd. I was getting stressed out.

"I tried to school her some while we were on the road," said Jim. "Did my best."

"Oh, that's great," said Mr. Brink. "Maybe we can find a place for you in the parent-teacher-student triangle. Maybe we can just make that the parent-teacher-student-*bum* rectangle!"

The desk part of the little desk, which Jim had been gripping too tightly, now broke off in his hands. He stood up. "Seems like this was a bad idea. I'll go."

"Oh, surprise!" said Mr. Brink. "Shocker! Go. Go ahead. Go and leave. That's all you ever do."

Jim held up the little broken desktop like a shield in front of his chest. "You still haven't forgiven me.".

Now we were getting some drama. If I'd been the producer of this reality show, I'd have been stoked. But since I was not a producer and was in fact a child watching two grown-ups fight, I was just uncomfortable. I realized that on some level I had been expecting that as soon as Jim and Mr. Brink got in the same room, they'd put their wrists together so their matching bracelets would line up and mystical rays would burst out of them and they'd be enveloped in a Double Rainbow–style halo of siblinghood and happy-ending-ness. But instead, the room was full of hurt feelings and dicey family dynamics that were none of my business and also slightly nauseating. I liked to think of Mr. Brink as a cool role model, an icon, and here he was acting exactly as lame and bratty as I must have seemed when Evan first told me I wasn't allowed in his room cuz his new friends were over. Then it hit me—the big, sad truth. Adults. They're Just Like Us. I shook my head.

Mr. Brink wasn't speaking again, and neither was Jim. So I intervened. "You guys, it's Christmas slash Hanukkah. Slash Kwanzaa. And Jim came all the way back here to spend it with you. The past is the past. History's important, but sometimes you have to let it go. What matters is family. What matters is love. That is what makes this country great." I would have kept going, just desperately throwing off-brand Disney Channel moral lessons out there hoping something would stick, but Jim stopped me.

"The kid is right," he said. "It's Christmas. We got a lotta talkin' to do. And I don't want to waste any more time. I'd like to spend Christmas with you this year. If you'll have me."

"No," said Mr. Brink.

Jim flinched. My eyes bugged out. No sound effects were heard, despite an obvious need for an exaggerated record-scratch.

"No," Mr. Brink repeated, "what I mean is—Christmas is not enough." He took a step toward Jim. "I need more than one day. I need you in my life. You're my brother, man. I need you to stay. Here. In town. You can crash on my couch. I'll help you get a job. We'll figure things out. But just don't leave again. Please."

I gaped at Jim. Mr. Brink had really upped the ante. I tried to imagine what it would be like if Stumptown Jim gave up the hobo life and settled down here in Charlottesville. Would he shave his beard? Get a pair of khakis? Work at a bank or something? It was extremely difficult to imagine. Even now, just standing in this classroom, Jim had an aura of motion about him. I swear, if you listened closely, you could hear the echoes of trains running through him.

There was another bulky pause that we would need to edit out in post. Then Jim said, "I'll think about it."

Mr. Brink rubbed his eyes. "Okay. Good."

Stumptown Jim goes, "I need some air." And he walked out.

I did a little tap dance, like, mission accomplished, even though I wasn't quite sure what had transpired. Mr. Brink hesitated, then put his hand on my shoulder. At which point the glass-paneled door burst open, and the entire sixth-grade class rushed in.

"Mr. Brink! Mr. Brink!" screamed Tessa, arms flailing. "Did she leave?! Is she back?! Where's your brother?! What's happening?!?! AAAUUUGHGHGHHGHGHHHH!!!!!" Tessa collapsed in a twitching heap below the whiteboard. All the other sixth-graders swarmed around me. I had to climb up on a chair just so I could breathe. Everyone was taking pictures of me with their phones and tweeting and texting about me.

"I thought you were dead!" screamed Emma, Tessa's new second-best friend.

"I heard you went to jail!" yelled Kevin R., the second-grossest dude ever after Toothpick Frank.

"I heard you're wanted in all fifty states!" Tessa moaned from the whiteboard area.

"Only forty-nine," I said, #humblebragging.

Mr. Brink took control of the situation. "Okay, everybody, calm down. Our classmate here has been on a pretty crazy adventure, but all that's behind her now. She's back at school and she has a *lot* of catching up to do. Because this is the real world. Where we do our homework. Right? Back to reality. Okay."

I didn't consider that to be Mr. Brink's most inspiring speech. The room suddenly felt very *room temperature*. A bell rang, and it was officially winter break. Everybody stopped taking pictures of me and started packing up their bookbags and zipping their jackets. Then I remembered something. "Wait!" I called out.

"What is it?" said Mr. Brink.

"The tiny turtle! Don't I get to give him a name?!"

"He's not our turtle anymore," said Mr. Brink. "He stayed with the fifth grade."

And I felt a kind of unaccountable grief.

———————————

Now I'm outside, in the school parking lot, waiting for my mom to pick me up. All the other kids have gotten picked up already, and the school doors are locked for the break. You'd think the kid who'd been missing for a year would be the one to get picked up first, but when I called my mom she was on the other line, and she said to just hang tight because she was on with a client and it would be a little while. I looked around for Stumptown Jim when I came outside, but I didn't see him anywhere. Mr. Brink's car is gone. I wonder if they'll really spend Christmas together. I wonder too if my brother will be in the car when my mom shows up.

It's freezing out here, but there isn't even any snow.

SERENA VAN DER HAMSTER

This Christmas was good but not great. I got a hamster, but then I dropped her on the kitchen floor and she died. RIP Serena Van Der Hamster. This is her obituary:

Serena Van Der Hamster, 3 months old, of the Baltimore Van Der Hamsters, passed away this Christmas Day in Charlottesville, Virginia, after falling (okay, being dropped) from a medium height. Miss Van Der Hamster was the heir to a great fortune, namely, the cage, water bottle, and wheel she inherited from her human family's former pet, the much-loved, true-blue, no-fuss-no-frills hamster Bob (deceased). For the brief time she lived in our house, Serena was an active member of the community, tearing up no end of newspaper and pooping with abandon. With her golden fur and well-stocked food bowl she was truly a glamorous hamster and, it must be confessed, a bit of a snob. Indeed she refused to even be handled by her young owner and was generally quite rude and haughty. Still, she in no way deserved her fatal fall and was definitely not dropped on purpose. Funeral services will be held this evening in the backyard, where Miss Van Der Hamster will be respectfully buried in a neon purple Skechers shoebox. Music to be provided by an iPod playing Rihanna's hit "Diamonds." Shine bright, Serena. Like a diamond in the sky. You will be missed.

Nothing is as meaningful as a handmade Christmas gift. For example, a handmade DVD box set of *Gossip Girl*.

⊰ CHRISTMUKKAH ⊱

Ever since getting trapped in the mine, Christmas is different for me. Because now I'd actually be *psyched* to get a lump of coal.

Something else is different now too. And I don't mean that my brother says I'm allowed to go in his room again. (Well, technically, *he's* not allowed to close the door of his room according to new rules set by my parents since he came back from rehab, but still.) It's bigger than that. And I can't talk about it with anyone.

I'm having trouble sleeping at night. Of course on Christmas Eve I just chalked it up to impending Haul-Video anxiety, but then I couldn't sleep on Christmas night, or last night either. The problem is this bed. It's too soft. Too frilly. And most of all—too *stationary*. I miss the road. The train—it has a sound. A feeling. And it gets to you. You get accustomed to it. Long as the train keeps running, you sleep like a princess—and soon as it stops, you wake up. Whereas here, in this house, in this room—I'm just tossing and turning.

I'd like to say that everything's back to normal since I came home, that the aliens who abducted my parents and replaced them with zombie duplicates have flown the white flag and restored everybody to their original human selves, but I'm not convinced that's the case. For the first twenty-four hours, there were a lot of demands for "big hugs"—but I never quite felt anyone's arms around me tightly enough. There was too much air in those hugs. And when my dad sat me down for a "serious talk" about my schoolwork, he couldn't maintain steady eye contact with me. His line of sight kept sneaking off to the side of my face, or up above my shoulder.

I don't trust these people, that's the problem. Not the way I came to trust my companions on the road. Funny thing about tramps, bums, and thieves—they're always breaking the law, but they have a foolproof sense of right and wrong. There are good people and bad people out on the road, and everybody knows the difference. The good ones take care of each other. They might do the wrong things, but it's for the right reasons, and it's at the right times. They have a code, and they abide by that code. Here, in this house, I never know what anyone's up to. I feel like everyone's hiding things from me—and if they're not, that might make it even scarier. Because then they're just, like—*voids*.

My mom made my brother paint over the place on his ceiling where he wrote, "Life is pointless." I stood in the open door-way while he was up on the ladder whiting it out. He looked old-fashioned, up on the ladder. It's kind of a classic, historical move—painting something. You can't do it on a computer. Any-way, I was watching him and he goes, "What?" And I go, "Are you painting over it because Mom told you to? Or because you don't believe it anymore?"

He didn't say anything. But when he climbed down off the ladder, he put his arms around me and squeezed. And it actually felt real.

I keep wondering how Stumptown Jim and Mr. Brink are doing, over at Mr. Brink's house on Jefferson Street (yes, I know where he lives, I stalk his Facebook). I wonder if Jim will agree to stay in Charlottesville, like a regular guy. What if he got a job at our school? Can you imagine? I'd be on my way to class and I'd pass Jim in the hallway, mopping or something. I don't know. I don't know if I'd like that. And I sure don't think that Jim would like it much.

Thing is, I was only on the road for a year, and I got this restlessness that won't let me sleep. Something tells me Jim's not sleeping well either. Something tells me, in fact, that if I were to throw this comforter off me and hop out of bed and pull on my UGGs and three sweatshirts and a fun winter hat and pack up my bindle and tiptoe downstairs and slink out the patio door and run and run and run all the way to the train tracks, Jim would be standing right there. Waiting for me. And we'd catch the next cannonball straight outta town and we'd be free as birds. But smarter and cooler because birds, I have come to learn, basically suck.

I tell you what. If I don't fall sound asleep in the next five seconds, I'm doing it. Five. Four. Three. Two. YOLO.

I can't wait to go back to hobo camp—my counselors RULE!!!!!

Tween Hobo @TweenHobo   12/29

In the future I will use a 3D printer to print out a collection of dusty artifacts from my travels.

....

Tween Hobo @TweenHobo   12/30

On the graves of my ancestors, I will never use Bing.

....

Tween Hobo @TweenHobo   12/31

Should old acquaintance be forgot you can probably find them on Facebook.

....

Tween Hobo @TweenHobo   1/1

JUST FOUND A FIVE-LEAF CLOVER, SO, PRETTY SURE I CAN MOVE THINGS WITH MY MIND.

....

Tween Hobo @TweenHobo   1/2

This year, I play my cards right, I get trapped in a museum.

....

Tween Hobo @TweenHobo   1/3

I'm making a digital short about Toothpick Frank: "Dick in a Boxcar."

....

Tween Hobo @TweenHobo   1/4

I call my backup husband Justin Case.

....

Tween Hobo @TweenHobo   1/5

You fell for that happy face? You just got emoticonned.

Tween Hobo @TweenHobo   1/6

Every day I give thanks for the clothes on my back, the food in my belly, and the celebrities who follow me.

Tween Hobo @TweenHobo   1/7

Lifehack: Always ask for more wishes.

Tween Hobo @TweenHobo   1/8

I'm DTF (Down To Fiddle).

Tween Hobo @TweenHobo   1/9

My upcoming book is like the *Lean In* of how to never get a job.

Tween Hobo @TweenHobo   1/10

Rough and toilsome week's at an end; now it's catch-as-catch-can for sleepovers.

⇥ JANUARY 11 ⇤

On the Road Again!!!

We're more than halfway to Chicago by now. Soon as we get there, we'll hop off, find an easy mark, and hook ourselves up with three hots and a flop (and hopefully some Wi-Fi). But for now, all we have to do is ride. Just lie back against the rusty walls of the boxcar and let the train carry us through this big country. Stumptown Jim's playing his guitar like the old days, and the whole gang's congregated: Tin Cap Earl, Toothpick Frank, Hot Johnny Two-Cakes, Salt Chunk Annie, Whiskey Bob, a couple of new guys, and me. I'm an old-timer at this point. I'm only twelve, but I'm a hard twelve.

Stumptown Jim gave me a book for Christmas. Just as we were pulling out of Virginia, he sprang it on me. It's a dusty, beat-up old book, with yellowed pages, and not even a picture on the front. It looks like part of a boring diorama. Immediately I got suspicious and thought Jim was trying to homeschool me again, but he explained that it was a gift, and he thought I might like it, because it's all about hobos. The OG hobo to be exact—a guy named Jack London, who rode the rails back in 1890-something and wrote down all his experiences, just like I did. I said, okay, cool, but can't I just download it on my Kindle? (I swear I got six different Amazon gift cards for Christmas, and my Kindle's right here in my Bindle™.) But Jim just laughed in that Stumptown Jim way and goes, "Sometimes it's nice to hold on to the real thing."

So I open the book to a random page and start skimming. I'm pretty sure it's above my reading level. But it's intriguing. Lots of gritty hobo details, which I appreciate. *We sprang to our feet and strung out alongside the track*, it says. *There she came, coughing and sputtering up the grade, the headlight turning night into day and silhouetting us into sharp relief. The engine passed us, and we were all running with the train, some boarding on the side-ladders, others "springing" the side-doors of empty box-cars and climbing in.* I nestle against Stumptown Jim to keep warm and munch on some kettle corn and feel like the credits are rolling and I'm okay with that. The book goes on:

Above me the stars were winking and wheeling in squadrons back and forth as the train rounded the curves, and watching them I fell asleep. The day was done—one day of all my days. To-morrow would be another day, and I was young.

Tomorrow will be another day, I think, and *I'm* a tween.

⋛ TOP TEN CAVES ⋚

It's time for me to make my year-end list.

Top Ten Caves I Hid Out in This Year

10. That One Cave with the Half-Empty Bottle of Root Beer
9. The Cave Where the Wolf Family Took Me In and We Exchanged a Best Friends Forever Necklace
8. The Cave Where I Ritualistically Set All My Math Homework on Fire
7. The Cave Where I Caught a Grown-Ass Werewolf Imprinting on My Baby Acorn Daughter and I Punched His Lights Out
6. The Cave Where I Found a Light Yellow Scrunchie That Was Just a Little Bit Dirty
5. The Cave Where I Launched My Small Salon Business Doing a French Braid in Toothpick Frank's Beard
4. The Cave Known as Beyoncé's Nursery Cuz It's Full of BLUE IVY
3. Capri Sun Cave (#SponsoredCave)
2. The Cave Where I Time-Traveled but Didn't Mess Anything Up So You Wouldn't Know about It

And the #1 Cave of the Year:

1. The Cave I Visited with My Time Machine in the Future Full of the Old Bones of Everybody Whoever Unfollowed Me

⋛ SPECIAL THANKS ⋚

As I traveled along the information superhighway, I met some nice folks who helped me out with a retweet or Rice Krispie Treat. So, when I die, I'd like for my slap bracelets to be divvied out equally among the following cool dudes: Stephen Burt, Shannon Opp Foster, Mariah Garnett, Peli Grietzer, Steve Hely, Dave Jargowsky, Liana Maeby, Joe Marianek, B. J. Novak, Sonia Paul, Jennifer Preston, Nathan Rabin, Richard Rushfield, Alexis Swerdloff, Jim Windolf, and Emily Yoshida. I bequeath my American Girl accessories and any unused portion of my Amazon gift cards to my agents, Alyssa Reuben and Chris Licata. To my editor, Jeremie Ruby-Strauss, my bindle. Nick Harmer and Hum Creative get my little American-flag knee-patches. Eben, Doug, and Jane Smith can keep my sticker collection. My BFFL forever is Emma Rathbone; she gets my tampons, assuming I died before I got my period. Finally, I wish to entrust some *very* romantic emoji to the only boy who is hotter than Hot Johnny Two-Cakes, Emilio Oliveira. Woop woop woop!